The Ups & Downs (plus more?) of Substitute Teaching

By
Wilhelmina Pinheiro

Bloomington, IN Milton Keynes, UK

authorHOUSE

7-2006

AuthorHouse™
1663 Liberty Drive, Suite 200
Bloomington, IN 47403
www.authorhouse.com
Phone: 1-800-839-8640

AuthorHouse™ UK Ltd.
500 Avebury Boulevard
Central Milton Keynes, MK9 2BE
www.authorhouse.co.uk
Phone: 08001974150

First published by AuthorHouse 5/5/2006

ISBN: 1-4259-1382-2 (sc)

Printed in the United States of America
Bloomington, Indiana

This book is printed on acid-free paper.

ACKNOWLEDGEMENTS

This book is a compilation of my own experience in the field of teaching and that of other learning processes that came across my way directly or indirectly.

The following people have contributed to this book indirectly but have not been quoted directly. I would like to thank all of them especially, Mr. Craig Warner, Director of AMERICORPS, Reno, Nevada; Mr. Jose Lara, Administrator of the United States Peace Corps, Dominican Republic; Mr. Gary Wyatt, State of Nevada; Ms. Florence Philipps, Nevada; Ms. Rosie Figueroa, State of Arizona; David Raulston, Vice President, Heald College; Mr. John Loo, State of Hawaii; Mr. David Roy, State of Rhode Island, and finally to Dr. Carol White, Principal, Rainshadow Charter High School for her invaluable editorial assistance.

To my Mother Rose, my Husband Albert who is my love, and my grandmother Lolah, my niece Marie – special thanks for their unfailing encouragement.

This book is dedicated to my
Love who, whenever I get home
would ask the same
question to me all the time
**"Tell Daddy, what happened
to my baby in school today."**

TABLE OF CONTENTS

PREFACE

WE ARE ALL SUBSTITUTE TEACHERS, whether one be a child, a mother, a sister, a brother, a grandparent, as a mother in-law, a neighbor, a friend, as a classmate, an enemy, a lover or a stranger.

As a child, one would teach her playmate to follow the rules of the game.

As a mother, one would teach her child to sit correctly, to stand up straight, to do housework, to respect her elders, to study hard and to be the best that she could be.

As a sister, she would teach her what she already knows from experience and to be able to protect herself from harm.

As a brother, he would teach her to play with him, be it a ball or a water gun.

As a grandparent, he would teach her the wisdom that was passed on to him in the course of time. The energy he exerted to be what he is now and to be the greatest person he could possibly be.

As a mother in law, she would teach him/her the likes and dislikes of her child.

As a neighbor, he would teach one to agree to disagree with his convictions.

As a friend, he would teach her the value of friendship

As a classmate, he would teach her to either be good or bad ; to gear him to the right direction or to lead him to the mud.

As an enemy, he would teach her the art of hating and criticizing

As a lover, he would teach her the beauty of love and affection.

As a stranger, he would teach her the strangeness of being weird or being different.

This development was logical and necessary. They all believed that we should be trained to take care of ourselves at all times and advance ourselves in the community around us. Teaching is an endless task. One can embrace what he learned and impart it to the next generation or to stop sharing his knowledge to make sure that no one gets the better of him. The teaching of the great philosophers is a product of our individual convictions. The beauty of the sky up above and the depth of the ocean is part of what was taught to us. We learned how to appreciate what we become or hate the result of what we came out to be. It is up to us to judge our neighbors, and our surroundings.
WE ARE ALL SUBSTITUTE TEACHERS!

INTRODUCTION

This book is packed with suggestions on what to do and what not to do while doing your work as a substitute teacher and in requesting for a sub.

Samples on attitudes of the students, the teachers, and the principal will be discussed in the following pages. Communication from the regular teacher to the substitute teacher will be illustrated in both verbal – non verbal communication.

Similarly, it is up to the regular teacher and the substitute teacher to look for cues to make it easy for the sub to perform his duties that would result in a satisfactory day for the students and for the returning teacher to pick up where he/she took off.

Daily practice of the regular teacher should be communicated in the lesson plan to offset misunderstanding from the sub and the students themselves. The quality of the performance of the sub depends on how well the regular teacher communicates with the sub whether orally or written via lesson plans. This reflects how knowledgeable and considerate is the regular teacher to the sub who will make it easy for both of them to produce a fruitful day for the teacher, the sub and the students.

Make a positive effort to make it easy for the sub to take your place. On the other hand, the sub should not be overwhelmed with worries and challenges surrounding his days because of what he heard from other subs as to how difficult are the students in some areas of the city.

Some principals and teachers unleash unthinkable atrocities to some substitute teachers basing their judgment from the perceived notions of other teachers and subs. All sorts of problems can arise from this issue if not resolved.

Take time to give feedback to the sub upon his return (if ever), and the sub to the teacher as well. People want to know how well they are doing. Compliment more than you criticize. A constructive criticism giving way for improvement is an area that is difficult to face. The secret of a good relationship between the sub and the teacher will be up to the both of them to waive a flag of either white or red.

Consequently, by bearing in mind that we all have our own ideas, it will prevent us from being in trouble in approaching complex situation whether it is with teachers, supervisors, or students. Challenges are part of life. It is up to us to accept accountability for our actions. When confronted with difficult situation, keep walking with your head high and kick the stones that block your way.

PART 1

The AGONY

The NEED

The DEFEAT

The TRIUMPH

THE AGONY –
THE CONNECTION /
DISCONNECTION

After qualifying to be a licensed substitute teacher, the sub starts to hope and to expect to be called in for a daily assignment.

Once the sub starts working, it is up to the sub to form his contacts by doing his best in the report that he turns in to the regular teacher regarding his performance. It would be wise for the sub to write a short note to the regular teacher where he could be reached for any questions regarding his report or for future assignments that may arise.

This is the time to form a list of the schools, location, names, subjects, and grade level where you have substituted. It is important to write a short note regarding your impression on that day and on that school.

When necessary, you may enter notes on the other teachers around the classroom where you are assigned and state if you made contact with other teachers in the same school.

Sometimes, it is best to give positive impressions in the report that you will turn in to the regular teacher if you feel that you wanted to be called again to take over in that particular class. It is equally important to be honest and tell your true impressions of the class especially if the class is really rowdy and that you do not wish to return to that particular class and do not wish to sub for that particular teacher again.

It is not only the teacher that you may wish to connect or disconnect. In many cases, the principal counts a great deal too. I remember having worked for a school where I was called to the office of the principal the following day.

I thought all along that I was called to sub again in that particular school. Much to my surprise, the principal asked me to sit down in her office and without hesitation asked **"why did you leave a rotten apple on the table of the teacher you worked for yesterday?"** I was stunned with this direct accusation without even asking me if I really left a rotten apple or not. The only thing I could say was this: "do you think I will risk my $110.00 daily salary by leaving a rotten apple on the table?" What hurts me about this accusations is the fact that I really enjoyed having worked for that teacher because her class was well behaved and her lesson plan was well explained. I left the office with a heavy heart and promised myself not to return to that school ever again. Later, I learned that the custodian was the one who left the rotten apple in that room intentionally for reasons of his own.

The sad thing after that incident is that there was a big workshop for all the teachers statewide the following week. The Department of Education tapped on all the subs but still the shortage was unavoidable. I received a call from a lot of teachers in that school after the Department of Education gave up on calling more substitute teachers as there was a great demand for subs. Although I have formed a list of friends in that school I refused to return and work there ever again. I have permanently disconnected myself in that particular school as I really lost respect for the principal.

As for the regular teachers way of disciplining the class, there are things that the sub should not overlook. One time I was asked to sub for a middle school in a nice area of town. The teacher has a unique way of disciplining her class. She wrote in the lesson plan the following.

Dear Sub, I have 12 students and I want to tell you that if you do not wish to be bothered with disciplining the students, you should take note of the following students: Jean sits by the window as she wants to watch the people go by. Peter sits by the door as he wants to watch his friends play in the yard. Johnny sits next to Joceline because she is his girlfriend. Joshua plays with his cards and shuffles them from time to time as he gets nervous if he does not work with his hands. Sean, Daniel and Joel are good friends and would like to be in one corner of the room by themselves. Let

them all do their own thing as they are all good students". Then she ended her letter to me with a drawing of a smiling face.

When I went home that day, my husband asked me how I liked the school where I was assigned to teach and I said to him: ***"I was not assigned to teach my love, I was assigned to baby sit instead".***

Here is another incident that I cannot forget, I was asked to teach an ESL, (English as a Second Language) class with four TA's (Teachers's Assistants). One was Chinese, one was Japanese, one was Spanish and one was Korean. Whenever I try to open my mouth to say something like introducing myself, to the students, one of the TA's came to me and said: "no need to do that because my group listens to no one but me." I was shocked with the way she approached me. Then, I tried to distribute papers that the teacher asked me to return to the students and one of the TA's grabbed it from me and said: "I will do that, I know who they are". Then I tried to sit myself in one corner so I can watch what each group is doing and the TA said to me: "No need to watch us, you will not understand us".

Finally, I just sat in front, and started to write my report to the regular teacher to be turned in late in the day. One of the TA's came to me and instructed me to erase the board because she had to write something later. I was disgusted and offended that day but made sure to put an asterisk in my list of contacts to make sure that I do not accept another assignment from this teacher.

There are students who want to get the attention of every one in the room and this can produce trouble for the sub most of all. I was asked to take my students to the auditorium to watch a program. When the students sat in one row assigned to my class, three students stayed away from the group, and since I am not familiar with their faces, I did not know that they separated themselves from the group. These three troublemakers became loud and disruptive. Someone approached them and warned them to behave. They did not; and so she asked them who was their teacher. These three students pointed to me from a distance and they were playing with the rubber bands on their hands making it to appear like a bow and arrow pointing to me. That someone approached me angrily and said to me: "you should be able to control your students".

I was shocked because I did not know her just as much as I did not know who were my students. Later, I asked one of my well-behaved students as to who was the one that approached me. The student said to me: "She is the Principal". So you see, she tried to warn them to behave and when she did not succeed herself, she started blaming me.

This is another incident that can be agonizing for a sub.

There are times when the teacher's instructions include asking the TA and student teacher for work. The sub becomes a complete stranger in the classroom making her appear like she is at the mercy of the TA or student teacher. This is another agonizing moment for the sub as he or she can become a laughing stock of the students when they see that the sub has no idea on what is going on in the classroom.

I feel that the regular teacher should be taught to consider the role of the sub. Thus, if the sub has no part in the learning process for the day, the students will have no respect at all for the sub.

My advice to the sub is to put a notation in your records not to sub for the said teacher again if you want to keep your sanity.

I am one person who wants to give myself a pat in the back for my accomplishment for the day. How can I tell myself that I accomplished something and earned my dollar for the day when I did nothing but beg my assistants to give me something to do.

There will be times when a visiting teacher is invited to demonstrate something to the students. In this case, the regular teacher would be notifying the sub to expect the speaker at a certain time. The notice may be written this way: Mrs. X will come this morning to demonstrate how to cook a certain dish. Let's say it is a Vietnamese food.

Mrs. X started demonstrating the a,b,c's of making this dish. While cooking, she would let the students try the dish now and then, to taste for correct spices that may be needed. What she forgot to specify to the students is that the spoon that was used to taste should not be returned to the dish to be stirred again. At various times, I observed this of her. And so during the time to try the dish as we were given portions in a dish, I refused to try it as I know that it was not done properly. It was the flu season at that time and most of the students were coughing and sneezing.

When I refused to try the dish, Mrs. X said to me: "why, it is not good enough for you"?

Of course I felt insulted and as an excuse I just said that I am supposed to take a medical test in the afternoon and I am not supposed to have an intake of any kind except water.

But of course, that is not true, but I did not want to hurt her feelings the same way she did me.

After that, she demonstrated the art of baking a cake and the same thing happened.

When the frosting was placed on top, the students kept licking the spatula with their tongue and sometimes with their fingers and put it back to the frosting that they were making. I am just so glad that I thought of a good excuse earlier and so this time I was not insulted for the second time. The regular teacher was informed of my indifference and so she personally called my attention to the effect when she saw me subbing for another teacher in the same school that same week.

Sometimes, the agony of a sub for being misunderstood can linger for a long time making it difficult for her/him to accept another assignment from a particular teacher, thinking that the same incident can happen again.

The younger students in the fifth or sixth grades can also give an agonizing day to a sub.

I remember vividly when a boy who was 11 years old asked me if I would send him to the office if he did not do his work. I said that it would depend on how this would happen.

He intentionally sat at the back of the room and refused to do the work that was asked of him to do. I approached him and asked him to join his group working on a certain project

He dared me to just send him to the office for misbehavior and so I did. While leaving the room, he yelled to me and said: "I'll be back in 5 minutes".

He was right, he was back in 5 minutes just as he warned me and told me that I can send him away again and he will be back again. So I did send him back and he was right. He was back again in 2 minutes this time. I blame the counselor for allowing this to happen and I learned later that – that particular student is a relative of the counselor.

I give up. I promised myself not to accept another assignment from that school. Not only from that teacher but, from that school because

I was afraid to encounter the same student for fear that he might even harm me.

Sometimes, when this kind of incident happens, the student is not asked to see the counselor. Instead, the security person is called and the security will talk to the student for a minute telling him to be good. That is it! He would walk away after saying that and of course, the student will just laugh insulting me that nothing really came out of my reporting him to the security.

These are incidents that can give a sub a very frustrated feeling. I blame the school for allowing things to happen and I once called the attention of the secretary to this effect and she said to me that the Principal is new and young and would like to be friendly with all the students. What else can I say except to shut my mouth and never to return to that same school again.

THE NEED

The same thing with your family, sometimes the mother of the house gets sick.

The grandmother or sister in law is called in to take the place of the mother that is sick so that the family will continue to be able to function.

The same with the school, sometimes the teacher gets sick or has to attend to the personal problem of the other members of the family, so a substitute teacher is called in to take his place.

With the introduction of high technology nowadays, teachers are now required to take classes in Information Technology, meaning – this is a valid absence by the teacher and again, a substitute teacher is called in to take his place.

Other needs may arise like the introduction of new government programs like the one introduced by President Bush called…"No Child Left Behind".

And so again, a substitute teacher is called in to take his place.

There are a number of reasons why a substitute teacher is called in to take over. Because of this, the Department of Education formed a central calling place for the regular teacher to report his/her absence on a specific date and to explain the subject and grade level for the need. Sometimes, the regular teacher would even leave a phone number where he/she could be reached if there were other questions that the substitute teacher needs to have answered.

Because of this need, the Department of Education, introduced a training program to prepare the substitute teachers in the performance of his duties as a sub. Each state has his own standards to comply for the person to be qualified as a substitute teacher.

The daily salary of the substitute teacher varies depending on the level of his education, training and experience as a teacher. The daily salary varies from $45.00 a day up to $ 150.00, and sometimes up to $200.00 a day.

There is a great need for substitute teachers that are qualified to teach almost in any subject. There will be times when regular teachers will not have the chance to prepare a plan if he or she did not plan on being absent on a specific date.

As a result, the teacher may be honest to the sub and tell her the truth that she did not have the chance to prepare a plan. On the other hand, there are teachers who are not humble enough to admit her non-preparation and would expect the sub to do some guessing on what to teach.

That is the reason why the need for a qualified substitute teacher is a must for many schools in the 50 states.

A teacher called me at the eleventh hour telling me that the substitute teacher who was supposed to sub for her called in sick. Since she personally knows me, she personally called me at home and admitted to me that she had no plan prepared for me and it was up to me to improvise on the lessons for the day.

This was a grade 3 level and the students were gifted. I asked the students to divide themselves into 4 groups consisting of 4 students in each group since there were 16 students in all. I gave each group a dictionary and made them pick their favorite 30 or more words covering a, b, c, d, e, f, in the dictionary. The next group covered g, h, i, j, k, l, and the next group covered m, n, o, p q, r, s, and the last covered t, u, v, w, x, y, z..

After this was done, I asked them to use the words in sentences and to make their own drawings of the chosen words like fingers, vase, etc. This was made to appear like a compilation of a real book of definitions and its descriptions. The students were inspired doing this as their creativity was challenged.

With this example, you can imagine how boring this day could had been for all if the improvised plan by the sub was not interesting and challenging enough for the gifted children. There is no getting around the fact that a qualified substitute teacher is very much in demand in a society that is focused on progress.

There are schools that are polite and welcoming to the substitute teachers. On the other hand there are also schools that treat their substitute teachers like 2nd class citizens.

One elementary school in the State of Hawaii gives out flyers to the sub when they report for work. This is what it says in the flyers:

> *WELCOME to our school! A substitute teacher has the complex task of temporarily coming into a regular teacher's classroom on short notice and carrying on instructions with a group of unfamiliar students. A substitute teacher is not an easy role to fill, but basic knowledge, skills of classroom management, basic instructional skills and your professional behavior must be implemented at the highest level possible. Our mission is to create an environment that fosters positive experiences which nurtures confident, well-rounded and successful students, eager to do their work and be the best they can be.*
>
> *Enjoy our children and have a wonderful and productive day! By: The Principal*

Then the 2nd page of this flyer states the Standard Operational Procedures to follow as a substitute teacher. Every school has its own hand outs on procedures to follow.

STANDARD OPERATIONAL PROCEDURES

❖ *Verify your substitute teaching assignment with the secretary*

❖ *Sign substitute agreement form*

❖ *Obtain classroom keys*

❖ *Lesson plan/assignment*

❖ *Check mailbox*

❖ *Report to classroom*

❖ *Open windows and lights*

❖ *Write your name on the board*

❖ *Locate attendance cards/seating charts*

❖ *Review lesson plans carefully and follow plans as closely as possible*

❖ *Do not use corporal punishment*

❖ *Do not leave students unsupervised in your class*

❖ *Maintain an orderly classroom at all times*

❖ *Correct all assignments as requested*

❖ *Complete your substitute form*

❖ *Secure classroom*

❖ *Return your keys*

In some schools, the bell schedule is the only thing they give out to the substitute but others would also include lunch schedule and their rules and regulations for students.

It is important for the sub to understand the rules of each school as each one of them can give you as a sub, their own rules and regulations.

Sometimes, the pass to be given to the student (if one wish to go to the bathroom) should not be written in a piece of paper. Instead, the student is given a key to the bathroom hooked up into a piece of wood (the size could be as big as a picture frame) to make sure that the key will be returned to the teacher and will not be taken home.

In the majority of schools where I sub, the attendance sheet should be marked with the symbols that they want you to follow: Example: To mark the absence of a student in the attendance sheet, the symbol used is a slash / and not the letter A for an absentee.

Some teachers use an X for an absentee and some teachers would also use the sign dash - for tardy which means that if a slash is marked already and a dash is added over it, that means that the student came in late.

Most of the high school bell schedule will give you various schedules depending on the days of the week. For example: On Mondays and Tuesdays, it is double periods.

On Wednesdays and Thursdays, shortened periods-which means early release for the students and on Fridays, it could mean something else.

There are teachers that will require you as a sub, to turn in your attendance sheet to the office within 20 minutes of the first period. On the other hand there are teachers who would specifically tell you NOT to turn your attendance sheet to the office. There are also schools requiring the security person to collect the attendance sheet from all the classrooms in the duration of the first period.

There are teachers who will warn their subs as to who are good and bad among students. They could be very specific. Example: Serafin is always picking a fight with almost anybody. Joshua is always teasing Annabelle. Make sure they are seated far away from each other. Other than that they are basically good students. Then they would end their notes with a happy face wishing the sub a very good day.

The subs do appreciate warnings of this kind as it will also help them avoid stress and anxiety and can act accordingly regarding discipline to be observed in the classroom.

BELL SCHEDULE

MONDAY

PD 1	8:02	-	8:51
PD 2	8:57	-	9:46
RECESS	9:46	-	9:56
PD 3	10:02	-	10:51
PD 4	10:57	-	11:46
LUNCH	11:46	-	12:26
PD 5	12:32	-	1:21
PD 6	1:27	-	2:16

TUESDAY

PD 1	8:04	-	9:21
RECESS	9:21	-	9:31
PD 2	9:37	-	10:54
PD 5	11:00	-	12:17
LUNCH	12:17	-	12:57
PD 6	1:03	-	2:20

WEDNESDAY

PD 3	8:04	-	9:21
RECESS	9:21	-	9:31
PD 4	9:37	-	10:54
PD 5	11:00	-	12:17
LUNCH	12:17	-	12:57
PD 6	1:03	-	2:20

THURSDAY

PD 1	8:04	-	9:21
RECESS	9:21	-	9:31
PD 2	9:37	-	10:54
PD 5	11:00	-	12:17
LUNCH	12:17	-	12:57
PD 6	1:03	-	2:20

FRIDAY

PD 1	8:03	-	8:57
PD 2	9:03	-	9:57
RECESS	9:57	-	10:07
PD 3	10:13	-	11:07
PD 4	11:13	-	12:07
LUNCH	12:07	-	12:47
PD 5	12:53	-	1:47
PD 6	1:53	-	2:47

ASSEMBLY SCHEDULES

TUESDAY, WEDNESDAY, THURSDAY
Back to Back Assemblies during B-C or D-E periods

Opening	8:00	-	8:04
Period A	8:04	-	9:12
Recess	9:12	-	9:22
Passing	9:22	-	9:27
Period B	9:27	-	10:27
Passing	10:27	-	10:32
Period C	10:32	-	11:32
Lunch	11:32	-	12:07
Passing	12:07	-	12:12
Period D	12:12	-	1:12
Passing	1:12	-	1:17
Period E	1:17	-	2:17
Closing	2:17	-	2:20
Opt. Act.	2:20	-	3:00

FRIDAY
Back to Back Assemblies during A-B, C-D, E-F or F-G periods

Opening	8:00	-	8:04
Period A	8:04	-	8:56
Passing	8:56	-	9:01
Period B	9:01	-	9:46
Recess	9:46	-	9:56
Passing	9:56	-	10:01
Period C	10:01	-	10:46
Passing	10:46	-	10:51
Period D	10:51	-	11:36
Lunch	11:36	-	12:11
Passing	12:11	-	12:16
Period E	12:16	-	1:01
Passing	1:01	-	1:06
Period F	1:06	-	1:51
Passing	1:51	-	1:56
Period G	1:56	-	2:41

THE DEFEAT - THE ATTITUDES /
THE CHALLENGES

It is not just the Teachers, the Principals, or the Teacher's Assistants that can aggravate your day. Most of the time the students themselves can get on your nerves.

After I called the attendance one day, one of the students asked me to give her a pass so she could go to the library and do her work there. She did not know that the teacher wrote me a letter telling me not to allow Sharon to go to the library if she asks for a pass. Therefore, I refused to give a pass to Sharon and told her to do her work in the classroom.

Sharon called her boy friend seated at the back of the classroom and said to him: "Aren't you going to do something about her?" The boy came to me and said: "give her a pass or else"....By this time, I asked one of the students to call the security. But before the security came, Sharon and her boy friend left banging the wall and the door. The impact of the banging made the screw to fall.

21

I explained what happened to the security and after the end of that day the security walked me to my car.

I was also asked to do yard duty on that same day. While watching, the custodian approached me and said: "students now are so different from the past….big body, small minds".

The following week, I was asked to teach a special education class. It is typical for this class to be small but I did not expect that only one would show up. It was an air-conditioned room and the student in front of me was a young boy about 13 years old. After looking around and seeing that no one else was coming, the boy said to me : **"Mrs. P, since it is only the two of us, why don't we have sex?"**

I was stunned and afraid at the same time but showed my cool by giving him a construction paper and asked him to draw something that he could see around the room. Then, I slowly walked to the door, hoping to find someone and luckily, one of the teachers passed by. I told her what happened inside the room and she told me that she knows the boy and not to be alarmed because his mother is a prostitute.

When I came home, my husband said to me: **<u>"Tell Daddy what happened in the school today".</u>** When I told him what happened, he laughed and said to me..."<u>you should really write a book</u>".

I was assigned to sub for a high school teacher but was made to be a clerk instead of being a teacher. How? The lesson plan left to me is shown below:

Periods 1, 2 and 3 —Mary is in charge; she is a student teacher; ask her if she needs assistance. (which I did and she insisted that she does not need my assistance),

Periods 4 and 6 —

- Move to the back of the room and make 29 copies of the attached Memo. Place one in each of the Department Members Box downstairs.

- Place a sticker next to each teacher's name on the back of the teacher's boxes downstairs. Stickers should be placed to the right of the name.

- Give Mrs. XYZ in Room 6A the note card for Mr. ABC

- File catalogs stacked on top of the filing cabinet in the department's office. Put them in alphabetical order by company's name. Discard old catalogs from the same company.

- If anyone returns video equipment, have Mrs. XYZ lock it up in her storeroom in Room 6A

This was how the lesson was written and I am so glad that I kept a copy to this day.

Just as I expected, the student teacher Mary, reported me to the regular teacher and she reported me to the principal that I did not assist Mary in any way and left all the teachings to her. The Principal sent me a letter asking me why I did not assist the student teacher.

I responded with a letter in the following page.

Dear Ms. Principal:

Thanks for giving me the chance to respond to the accusation of the student teacher.

To begin with, when I came in and saw the lesson plan (attached) making Mary, the student teacher, to be in charge, I felt that it was a slap in the face but I went along with the teacher's instruction

For the umpteenth time, I asked Mary if there was anything I could do. This question was asked in each and every room where we went. Each time, her reply to me was this: "just stay around and read the newspaper," which was on top of the table anyway, so I perused the morning paper. She also suggested that I bring magazines the next day since it was a 2 - day assignment. Again, I told her to just let me know if there was anything I could do for her and she said: nothing since she said that she knows the students anyway.

At this time, I was forced to tell her a previous experience I had with an intermediate school putting T.A. in charge also. I told her that even showing a Video, I was not allowed to do, because the T.A. claims that she knows where they stopped yesterday. Mary gave this input to my story and I quote: "the nerve of that T.A."

So with this experience, I wanted to make sure that it does not happen again. After that story, Mary came to me and asked me if I could go to the backroom and administer SAT test to one student (Joshua) I did so without hesitation. During the assembly, Mary said to me that we have to go to the auditorium and so we did. I sat in the same assigned row with the students. Mary was seated next to me and we discussed the show afterwards.

Then, I was sent to another room, to be with another student teacher per the request of another teacher. I told this new teacher who asked me to go to another room that I was just a decoration in the room where I came from. I told her that Mary was very competent, (as I am always praising new student teachers because I know how difficult it is to start a new career).

This new teacher that requested my presence in the other room told me that I should not feel bad for not being able to do anything to help out because the school has to simply make sure that there is a certified teacher in the room which was also reiterated to me by Mary too.

In the afternoon Mr. ABC asked for my assistance in giving his SAT test. I did not hesitate to help again. I was the one who read the directions while he gave out the booklets.

Now, the filing part, I followed the lesson plan asking me to put in alphabetical order the company's name that was stacked on top of the filing cabinet and so I did. But while I was about to do this, the student teacher, Mary said to me that I should leave it on top of the cabinet instead. And so I showed her the lesson plan that I was asked to do this in alphabetical order. She said to me: "you have done it in alphabetical order alright so that's it. That is the reason why I put a checkmark in each item of the lesson plan after each time the direction is completed.

I asked Mary what she thinks of Mr ABC with me helping him out. She said to me: "He is nice, only that lately, he promised to put me in charge and that is not how it has always been."

So you see, Ms. Principal, it seems like there is no pleasing Mary. I can go on and on. I shared some of my teaching methods with her, my ups and downs as a teacher of 20 years wanting to help her out and this is what I get in return? Also, when she said that she thinks I am hesitant to help her out – please bear in mind that – that is a matter of opinion of a lay teacher.

Finally, all I can say is thanks for allowing me to say my piece. Please find the lesson plan attached then I signed this letter

I received a call from the Department of Education at about 7:30 in the morning while I was still on bed, asking me to teach at a certain high school. I usually get a teaching assignment the night before but since this school is near my house, I accepted it right away and without dilly-dallying, I reached the school in half an hour after the call.

I reached my classroom (after my visit to the office) at about 8:15. I looked for the lesson plan and found none. I went back to the office and reported this. The secretary told me to check with the teacher, Ms. X next door. Ms. X and I looked all over the room and found none. She told me to write it up in my report. After half an hour the regular teacher that was supposed to be absent walked into the room with the lesson plan when I was already explaining an improvised lesson for the day.

She handed me a plan asking me to explain Chapter 8 of the textbook. How can I explain a topic that I haven't even read myself? She said that it should be easy for all I have to do is to read it first and then explain. She did not realize that the students would be left with nothing to do while I do my reading. After glancing at the book and found it to be self explanatory, I asked the students if they want me to read the lesson orally or for them to read it quietly. We took a vote and the majority decided to read the lesson quietly. I emphasized though that if anyone has any question, he/she should come to me so I can explain it. A few came to me and I helped them. It is such a good thing that it was a topic that I like teaching. The subject was accounting. The plan did not specify what to do next. So, I decided to make them do a worksheet based on what was explained in the book and then I asked the students to make a ledger and a journal entry.

That was how I handled this class but supposing that I had no accounting background and another sub had been called to sub this subject, how could a sub work on a lesson that is completely unknown to him? A teacher can be more considerate to the sub as this can result into a feeling of defeat, displaying her ignorance to the students around him or her.

THE TRIUMPH - THE FEEDBACK

Once the students get to be comfortable with the sub, and that the sub has gained the confidence of the students, the sailing could be smooth on both ends.

There was a time that I was given a two (2) month assignment to sub in a high school level. Most of the students were boys in the senior level. They were already used to my daily approach on the subject to be discussed.

One day, Peter did not do his homework and so jokingly I said to him that if he does it again, I will spank you in your butt.. Then the student behind him quickly said to me:

"ME TOO MRS. P.,...ME TOO!".

It is important to make the students get to be comfortable with the sub and once the sub can prove that he/she knows his trade, things will run smoothly in the classroom and will gain the respect of each and everyone of your students. I remember showing them the respect that they deserve and the kind words uttered each day can go a long way into the mind of the young students. They want learning to be fun and so I believe in the Japanese Proverb which is "One kind word can warm three winter months".

Share your humor with your students. Gain their confidence by showing them the art of learning and the importance of making big dreams. Dreams that can make them reach to the top.

Share your interest and enthusiasm with your students. Make them feel that they are the shaper of the future. Make them believe that if they succeed then you will be proud to say: "He/she was my student" and it will be music to your ears when you hear him say" "I owe everything that I know from so and so. Do not forget to illuminate the lives of others. It gives them hope and brightens their day.

The great philosopher Buddha taught us that thousands of candles can be lighted from a single candle. Fun never decreases by being shared. Establish a good relationship with your students. Respect them and they will accord you the same respect you have given them. Make each day a memorable day that they learned something new from you and they had fun while doing it.

When trust is given to me as a sub, I want to be able to do more for the school and the students. One day, I was asked to sub for Mrs. A and my first period was to show a video to the students that would cover the whole period. I only had four students in that class. The teacher next door, Mrs. B, approached me and asked for help to allow her five students to join my class so she could cover another class where the teacher was absent. I gladly welcomed the five students to watch the video together with my own students.

After that period Mrs. B., came again and asked me if it was true that I used to work for Barbizon Modeling School. I said 'yes". She quickly asked me if I could help her 3rd period students to put on their make-up as they are all participants in the program set for noon program in the auditorium. She said that since I have a small class that day, she will be happy to take them under her wings and she will take full responsibility to Mrs. A. I had to agree and took over her 3rd period teaching them how to apply make-up and how to dress themselves. The students were very happy and comfortable with my intervention. I could see in their faces how much they appreciate my help. I received a "thank you" note from both Mrs. A and Mrs. B as I found out that they are very good friends with each other and they are always willing to help each other in many occasions in the past.

It was a busy day for me jumping from one student to another, dressing one after the other, making sure that they are ready for a great performance is a task that I enjoy doing.

It was music to my ears to hear them all calling me and saying…."I need help Mrs. P;…

"Please look at me Mrs. P….Tell me what's wrong with me Mrs. P….I don't like how I look Mrs. P….please tell me what's wrong…. ..how do I wear this Mrs. P…." .

It was a delight to work for students like them as I felt a personal triumph that day..

At this time, I was asked to teach second grade students in an elementary school. The lesson called for card making for different occasions. I wrote on the board the different occasions that they could choose to work on for their cards. I have enumerated the following: Christmas card, thank you card, birthday card, graduation card, anniversary card, etc., Much to my surprise, most of the cards they made, (9 out 12 students) was a "thank you card". To top it all, they were addressed to me with the message written like this: "thank you Mrs. P. for not shouting...thank you for helping me" etc....One of the students left this picture (below) on top of my table.

These gestures make me feel that I have earned their trust and respect. I had to put five stars in my record book for the teacher that I subbed for in that school for I wanted to see the students again whenever given the chance to do so.

The stress and anxiety brought to a sub, can lead into an unexpected turn of events.

One day, after looking for the attendance sheet and not being able to find it (after looking for it all over the room) three or four students walked into my room pretending and insisting that they belong to the class. They tried to create trouble. I ignored them like they were not around. Luckily, one of the teachers passed by and recognized the four students who happened to be known troublemakers. He asked them to leave right away and they left immediately.

After school, they approached me and said to me that they were just trying to see if I would lose my cool and yell at them like the other teachers or call the security. They apologized and even tried to help me carry my brief case.

After that incident, those four students became my friends every time I went to sub in the same school. They were most respectful and helpful to me and would even build me up with the other students.

One day, these four students were in my classroom. I had the attendance sheet with me that day and got to know their real names. They were eager learners and very motivated.

One of the students in the classroom tried to play smarty with me and one of my four newly found friends put a stop into the misbehavior of the smarty one.

Another incident happened that morning. Robert sat quietly in front of the classroom.

Then, Stanford came over and asked Robert to move. Robert did not wish to move. His reason was that there was no permanent seat assignment anyway. Stanford was persistent so this started a fight in the classroom. One of my four friends stood up and said, don't you have any respect for Mrs. P. who is just watching you – not wishing to side with anyone of you? The two stopped fighting wondering what happened to the four who used to be known troublemakers in the classroom.

"Despite everything, I believe that people are really good at heart."…. Anne Frank.

Wouldn't you agree? Challenges in doing substitute teaching can come from the regular teacher himself.

What do I mean by that?

A certain teacher left her teaching position in the middle of the term. She accepted another position in the same school as a coordinator. Let us call her as Mrs. X. The school had a hard time looking for a long term substitute teacher because Mrs. X would always be warning all the subs to expect a lion's den when they come in. She was right. It was really a lion's den as soon as you go into the room.

However, since they are senior students, I tried to swing to another approach of teaching by asking them to write in a piece of paper what they plan to do after graduation. I only required one or two sentences from them. Since it was not a heavy assignment, they all complied.

And then I made them play a game, the same game found on Lesson Plan # 2 of this book. After the game, they started to trust that I am there to gear them in the right direction to follow after they graduate. So you see, it is important for the students to trust you before they can embrace your way of thinking.

Show them that you are interested to see them succeed in life. Ask their point of view.

Remember to enjoy meeting people if you want them to have a fine time meeting you.

PART 2

THE SUBSTITUTE TEACHER AT WORK
SERVING AS A CARETAKER TO AN
ABSENTEE TEACHER AND GIVING BIRTH
TO THE IDEAS OF THE STUDENTS BROUGHT
TO HIS ATTENTION BY WAY OF
LESSON PLANS

THE SUBSTITUTE TEACHER AT WORK

The sub starts the day by reporting to the office of the school where he or she is assigned to work. After picking up the keys to the room and materials left in the cubby hole of the regular teacher, the sub is ready to go to the room, turn on the light, open the windows and familiarize herself to the materials in the room that the regular teacher may have left for her to read, distribute or copy on the board. Make sure to read all the materials at hand and around you then write your name on the board for the students to know how to address you.

Samples of the standard instructions given to the sub by the regular teacher would be explained in the following pages.

Please note that the regular teacher would sometimes write a detailed lesson plan for the sub. On the other hand, some may also just scribble instructions in a scratch paper making the sub guess what to do at a certain time or on a certain period. It would be up to you also to guess the free period of that particular teacher.

In the following pages, you will see how organized one teacher could be. You will also see how many expectations that he may have on the sub. At times, you will discover that the regular teacher is the lazy kind expecting all her TA.s (Teacher's Assistant) to do all the work for her.

The ideal teacher to sub for is one who knows that a sub is stranger and considered by the students as an intruder. Because of this, the regular teacher would write instructions clearly stating to the sub the kind of students to expect. For example: The students written in the attendance list with asterisk next to name is the student that is most familiar with the plans for the day and that if the sub is at a lost on the comings and goings in the classroom, this is the one person that can clarify things for her.

Teachers may be considerate or not. Because of shortage of teachers, sometimes the Department of Education would call on a sub even though that is not the field of her/his expertise. For example: I was asked to sub for an automotive class. I had no knowledge of this subject but the regular teacher that I sub for one day told me not to worry because all that I had to do was play a video tape on how to change the oil and tires. His next instruction to me was to tell the students that he would give a test on this subject when he returns. This is one teacher that I commend for understanding the fact that subs are called to maintain peace in the classroom and still make sure that they learn something from the sub on the day of his absence.

SAMPLE 1 - LESSON PLAN

This lesson plan was written by a high school teacher:

Period 1 - Take the class to the computer room next door to room 226 for the first half of all the periods today starting at 8:30 AM.

Read "The Wolf" then, ask the students to answer the questions after reading the chapter and tell the students to write the answers in complete sentences on their folder paper.

Period 2 - Go to the gymnasium and attend the play presented by the senior class. Sit at the assigned area only. The teacher attached a map in his plan.

Period 3 and 4 - same as period 1

Period 5 - Your time to prepare for the next period - time to relax.

Period 6 - Same as period 2

NOTES:

1. Geraldine Santos of Period 3 would insist on sitting at the table by the teacher. Let her, as she would fret if you ask her to join the rest of the class.

2. Peter in period 4 would insist on distributing the folder to his classmates. He wanted to be helpful. Let him.

3. Allison enjoys chewing gum blowing bubbles to call the attention of others. Let her.

4. Do not be surprised if James will kick the rubbish can on his way out. Ignore him. Do not call his attention to the effect as he was always looking for a fight.

ASSESSMENT, PLAN 1

When the teacher allows the student to do whatever he chooses in the classroom, the teacher becomes the follower, meaning the student might as well be the teacher.

The attitude of giving in to the wrong doing of the student will lead to destroy the confidence of the rest of the students. Learning will not take place.

Rearing the children may be compared to lighting a candle. After you light a candle you will see the wax dripping too much on one side; you try to trim it so that the candle will continue to burn straight up and not bend on one side. The same with a child, he has to be trimmed accordingly for his own good.

SAMPLE 2 - LESSON PLAN
This plan was written by a high school teacher

Periods 2 and 4 & 6 - Take the students at the Conference Room in the Library for Career Workshop.

- Divide the students into groups of five (5 tables). Place a chart on each table. The speaker would distribute 12 cards to each table. Each card was written a certain profession and students were asked to give each card to the speaker when needed.

The speaker says: "In this chart you will see a jungle in the Amazon and as we go on finding the tree that cures cancer` we need help from different professionals as we go along the way"

- Each group would give one card (one profession) as the speaker asks what profession is necessary to tackle the problem. Example "Before we go to the jungle we need help to show us the way – who can help us?" ANSWER: Tour Guide or Park Ranger.

- The scorer would place one point for that group and if the next group will answer incorrectly just beep them without a point which would mean that they lost one card . This card might be necessary for the other questions along the way. The group that would receive most points will win and cookies will be awarded.

This is one way to familiarize the students with different professions to make them know if they wish to pick that particular career in the future.

MATERIALS NEEDED:

Index cards – with various fields written in the cards.

Markers – may be in different colors

Chart – in this case, jungle chart

Score card

ENDURING UNDERSTANDING:

To gain understanding of what field the students would like to consider as their career. This would guide them to make sure that they would be happy with their own choice.

The teacher could help the students by giving them sources of information on what was out there. He would also lead the students in making the right decision of what to venture or not to venture.

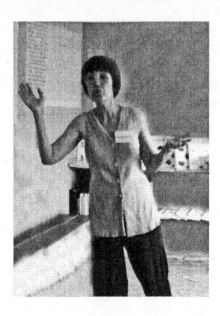

SAMPLE 3 - LESSON PLAN

This lesson plan was written by an elementary school teacher; grade level 2

1. Start the day by reciting the pledge of allegiance.

2. Ask the leader for the day, (Sharon), to take over and do the regular chores a leader does daily.

The leader made the students sit on the carpet. She made sure that the students formed a circle and she positioned herself in the middle of the circle. Then she started telling the rest of the class to focus. She is the only one seated on a small plastic chair in the center of the circle then she started with this introduction:

"Since I am the leader for today, I will start the discussion........
            "Last night, I ate pizza, any question? "
Peter raised his hand and asked this question:
            "What kind of pizza?"
Sharon replied: Pepperoni, any other question?"
Marlene said: "where did you eat your pizza?"
Sharon replied: "At Pizza Hut, any other question?"
Joseph asked: "who was with you?"
            "My father, any other question?"
Marcia asked: "Why did you go out to eat?
            "Because it is my birthday' any other question?"
"Who else was with you," asked Peter.
Sharon replied: "No one else, because my Dad told me not to tell anyone because he is cheap, any other question?"
"Did you finish the pizza?" some one from behind asked and Sharon replied:
            "No, my Dad asked for a doggie bag and he took it to work today".

After this discussion, Sharon said to me… "how do you like our presentation Mrs. P?"

I must admit that I was very impressed with the exchange of questions and answers by the students and made me believe that this teacher that I am subbing for was very smart and she made sure to give freedom to the students and let them know the meaning of responsibility. After this presentation, the rest of the day was easy as the teacher gave me the instructions on what else to do the rest of the day.

ESSENTIAL QUESTION, PLAN 3

What can we learn from this discussion?

With this exchange of questions and answers, I was impressed with the way Sharon presides the class and acted like a teacher herself gaining confidence speaking in front of the class and confident that she was in command on the floor.

How many times have we seen children in the lower grades, and mind you, even in the upper grades level, students are timid and shy to come forward and speak in front of the class. The training can start while we are young.

Never doubt that asking questions can lead to great discovery, and creative reasons and ideas may determine positive action perceived in a child's mind.

SAMPLE 4 - LESSON PLAN

This plan was written by a grade 7 Teacher –

Periods 1,3,5 and 7 - Tell all classes to read (orally by taking turns after each paragraph) Chapter 24 to 27 of the book – "The Giant Apple".

After oral reading, pass out the 3 page worksheet that I placed on top of the table and tell them to answer the questions up to the bottom of page 2 and we would discuss page 3 when I return on Wednesday. Collect their work- finished or not finished.

Period 6 – Tell the students to read a story in the magazine "Scope". After reading a story chosen out of the five stories in the magazine, change the ending of the story using the 20 new words that we learned last week.

Should there be time, they may work on their descriptive phrases

After finishing their descriptive phrases, ask them to use those descriptive phrases while they change the introduction of the story that they have just written. In other words, they have to turn in a different introduction and ending of the said story.

ENDURING UNDERSTANDING, PLAN 4

The students will learn to put a smile to a happy story or tears for a sad one. Creativity is the main ingredient in this lesson.

It takes a creative teacher with great imagination to make the students improvise on a story and learn how to apply it in their own lives.

Guiding the students to what they want to do with their lives will make them click and will produce a huge dividends to their future.

SAMPLE 5 - LESSON PLAN

This is an ESL, (English as a Second Language) class. The teacher is Vietnamese.

Periods 1, 2, 4 & 6 – Ask the students to share as much information of themselves to the class. Call them one by one to come to the front of the class and do a 2 to 3 minute talk on "Getting To Know You"

Notes from the substitute teacher:

Students were mostly from Vietnam and Thailand. They were very well behaved!

They could not utter the last consonant in a word. Example, eigh for eight. I had a hard time understanding them but got used to it by the end of the period. I tried to demonstrate the way their mouth should appear to express the consonant at the end of each word.

They were all appreciative of the lessons I taught them. I could see the big difference after I overly showed to them with my mouth wide open positioning my tongue correctly to be able to express the consonant.. I noticed that they understood the efforts I took to make my point across to them. Almost all of them came to me at the end of the class to say "thank you" and "good bye" at the end of the period. When I saw them later at the auditorium, the girls touched me on the elbow and some of them touched me on the shoulder – a sign of admiration and appreciation. They all spoke little English and I can tell that they were all eager to learn.

A very rewarding day!

CHALLENGE

Never doubt that a sincere desire to help one student to overcome his inferiority complex for being different from the rest of his friends will make a great impact to the attitude of that student. How much more helping a group of students?

Communication will give way to a great impression. If one is ashamed of the way she speaks thinking that everyone is watching her as she makes a fool of herself, how do you expect him to gain confidence communicating with the rest of the world?

It is an accepted theory that we form conclusion about people within seven seconds of meeting them. We form decision on their education, social status, honesty and integrity.

Teaching the students to gain confidence in imparting themselves and expressing themselves in a correct way will result in them gaining confidence in facing a challenging world

SAMPLE 6 - LESSON PLAN

This lesson plan was written by a grade 3 teacher

1. Start the day with the Pledge of Allegiance

2. Collect their homework.

3. Ask the students to display their work (drawings) with a clothes pin in the clothes line hanging across the back of the classroom.

4. Time for DEAR which means (Drop Everything And Read). Students know the drill. They would pick up a book on top of the counter at the right side of the room and they would start to read for 5 minutes.

5. After reading, they would pick up their folder in the cabinet to write a summary of what they read.

6. Time to open their worksheets on Arithmetic. Tell them to turn to page 12 and solve the problems on page 12 and 13.

7. Recess time - before they leave the room, ask them to turn in their work in Arithmetic.

8. After recess time, students would drop their head on their desk appearing to sleep; this moment would calm the students as they listen to music-harp, from a cassette tape played by the teacher for five minutes.

9. Students would pick up two construction papers for each one of them to be able to create something artistic that they could hang tomorrow at the clothes line if they get a grade of A. and the sub may ask the students to use all the remaining time before lunch time.

10. After lunch, Maria will turn on the cassette tape so that the class could listen to the music which is harp played in the cassette. Another calming time to beat stress. This will last for three minutes.

11. Ask the students to write some of the most unforgettable experiences they have experienced. Fill up the whole folder page.

12. Ask the students to read their work if there is enough time before dismissal time.

Make the students put up their chairs on top of the table to make it easy for the custodian to clean the room by the end of the day.

ORGANIZATION

It is obvious that this teacher should get an A plus for organizations. She knows how to blend learning from thinking and pleasure from learning.

This teacher would like to make sure that students know the value of time and management of time. She is instilling in them how to divide their time and to give way to learning and relaxation.

A good teacher knows that learning to organize time at an early age will guide them to be a good manager and not just a follower. Dividing time to meet your needs make them learn the value of time. Organization is a key to improvement leading to success.

SAMPLE 7 - LESSON PLAN

This lesson plan was written by a high school teacher

1st Period - This group would work independently. Have them read chapter 2 of the textbook Remind them to read quietly. When they are done, have them get the chart down and add two more conflicts/resolutions. Ashley should write in pencil. If they are done early they may work on their newspaper hunt.

2nd Period - The students needed to work on their Unit test in their Social Studies book on pages 50 - 52. Have them work with the person on their own table. They should not move unless they have no one else on their table then tell them to join Avery and Mike. Once they were done have them review the Study Guide that I have prepared for them and tell them to be sure that they can answer those questions for the test tomorrow.

3rd Period – The students would need to work on the Study Guide that I have prepared for them. They need to use their book to answer the questions. They must work with the person on their table they may not move unless they have no one else on their table then tell them to join Ashley.

4th Period – The girls could use this time to prepare for their play. It is required that they do a play for us. They could change the ending of the play in their book to make it better and more interesting.

5th Period - free period

6th Period - Same as Period 1

ASSESSMENTS

This is a teacher who knows how to discipline her students. They were very respectful and very independent in their learning process.

They were well trained to follow the instructions and guidelines given to them from the start of the school year. It is important to make sure that the teacher was to be respected by the students depending on the trust he gives them As a consequence the students would work harder to prove that they could be depended upon.

A rewarding day for everyone

SAMPLE 8 - LESSON PLAN

This lesson plan was written by a grade 8th teacher

(I have been subbing for her for quite sometime and she   knew me personally. She knows that I have a good knowledge of improvisation and so she asked me to give a short lecture on improvisation before doing the plan)

All classes in the morning – After you give your lecture on improvisation, ask the students to read "Read Magazine" aloud. Give the students parts to play on 3 Musketeers and ask them to do a play. This will be in preparation for the school play to be held next week. Grade them 1 to 5, five being the best.

Two Periods in the afternoon – Have the students clear their desks. Give them the Speed test. Multiplication – 5 minutes. After the test, ask Bradley to call out the answer and Romeo should put the scores onto our chart. Collect the speed test.

Ask the students to work on their journal, as I would be collecting them tomorrow.

CHALLENGE

The students were challenged to be able to think on their toes. Improvisation would produce creativity and creativity would lead to success.

If students are trained in the early years to think quickly and come up to a decision on what to do at a certain situation, this will make them become good thinkers and they can see for themselves that they will enjoy the opportunity of being given the chance to tend for themselves.

Learn to arouse the interest of the students. Give examples on the many ways to make them succeed in life if you want them to meet their challenges.

SAMPLE 9 - LESSON PLAN

This lesson plan was written by a high school teacher – Subject: ESL

Periods 1, 3 - Ask the students to work on the puzzles attached.

After 15 minutes, collect those puzzles and pick up 10 words from each puzzle.

Write them on the board and ask them to use those words in a sentence. After they have used those words in a sentence ask the students to work as a group of 4 or 5 and write a story using those sentences they have constructed.

The story should have some drawings and should consists of some 5 or 6 pages

Therefore, you can ask one student in each group as to who is the artist in their group and assign him or her to do the drawing that pertains to their story. For example: The hurricane destroyed the house of my neighbor. The picture that can be drawn is that of a house without a roof as it was blown by the wind and the strong banging rain.

Collect their work.

Periods 2 and 5 – Ask the students to work on their book "Skill Sharpeners".
Help the students understand the difference between 1st person and 2nd person.

Give some 20 examples.

ASSESSMENTS

Most of the students are Vietnamese. They were made to demonstrate their enthusiasm in the new language that they were learning. They would start to gain confidence and create new friends.

Students should be encouraged to keep on learning and make them understand that they have to do their own growing. No one can help them but themselves.

The interest that they will be showing is a good sign of their desire to be their own person and be a part of a conventional society.

SAMPLE 10 - LESSON PLAN

This was written by an ESL (English as a Second Language) teacher

Periods 1, 3 - Students were asked to read "The Wall", War in Vietnam. Students were working on three different levels. I have a T.A. for each level. Ask them to help out the students who could have questions regarding their readings.

Make the T.A. go over directions with the students making sure they understand the material they were reading and know what to do. Assist the students as needed, with their work. Check the exercise they have completed, mark their errors which students should correct and initial their work when completed. Do not allow the students to copy from each other.

Make sure that the T.A. (teachers assistant) would go around and assist as many students he could handle. This is a big class and the students need all the help they can get. Collect their work at the end of each period.

Period 4 – Students are to read "Read Magazine" aloud. Please help them if they encounter difficulty in reading. Use one of their own folder paper, ask them to answer questions on pp 16 to 17. Answers to the questions are attached. Please correct their work after class and put them on top of my table.

Period 5 – These students are gifted and advanced in their lessons. They were working on a speech that they were to present to the monthly meeting of their club for the gifted students. Help them, and give them pointers on how to catch the interest of the audience.

ENDURING UNDERSTANDING

Whether the students are gifted or not, knowing that they are taught to believe that there is always room for improvement inspires them to go on learning.

They should not be afraid to make mistakes. For some, speaking in public create sweaty palms. Practice in front of a mirror no matter how bad you may appear to be.

There is nothing wrong with you pausing now and then when you speak before an audience. If you appear to be grasping for words, do not worry - this is very common even with the best speakers.

It would merely justify the thought that you wanted to convey your ideas from your heart. You wanted to make your audience feel that the words you use comes from your heart.

SAMPLE 11 - LESSON PLAN

This is an English Class in the high school level

All Periods - A student was assigned in each period to take roll. Others were to pass out any materials needed like notebooks, journals etc and they know who they are and were very helpful.

Students have written the definition of PERSONALITY TRAITS in their notebooks. They were made to choose what best describes themselves and highlight them on their worksheets. Ask monitors to pass out the notebooks and folders. Under PHYSICAL CHARACTERISTICS they could measure height and weight and listed their eyes and hair color. Referring back to their notebooks and worksheet, they were to begin to write a paragraph that describes them such as

> MY NAME IS MARIE. I AM 5' 2" TALL AND WEIGH 100 POUNDS. I AM A VERY HAPPY PERSON. I DON'T EVER THINK THAT I AM UNHAPPY. I AM ALSO A VERY HELPFUL PERSON. I LIKE TO HELP MY CLASSMATES AND WHEN I AM HOME ...ETC.

Please feel free to model yourself - using yourself as an example. When students are finished, they can take turns reading their paragraph in front of the class.

CHALLENGE

With the example that the teacher made, I have reinforced to the students to challenge others and show to them that they were unique in their style. They should not necessarily have to start with I am this or I am that.... as a kindergarten student can do the same. Use your imagination and believe that your style is different from others.

You would like to catch the attention of the audience by starting your speech with the unexpected. Make the audience remember you for what you said of yourself.

You can start by asking your audience a question. For example: How many fingers do you have? Raise them up. As they raise them up you can say that when you took a typing course, your teacher told you that you have only 4 fingers in each hand.

You may continue by saying this: "My teacher said to me that my pointing finger is my strongest finger and that is my number 1 finger as I use it in so many ways, compared to my pinky, my number 4 finger as I use it only to poke on my nose and my ears. Since then I gave more attention to my number one finger and I always make sure to keep it clean and manicured. Then you can add more to this introduction now that you have gained the attention of your audience.

SAMPLE 12 - LESSON PLAN

This lesson was written by and elementary school teacher

8:00 – 8:30 – morning activities including the pledge of allegiance

8:30 – 9:30 – ask the students to turn in their homework and to read to the class their new year's resolution. Ask them why it was important to write down their new year's resolution. As an assignment ask the students to classify their resolution in three different levels. Example: personal resolution, school works resolution and family resolution.

9:30 – 10:00 – Ask the students to continue to work on their construction paper which they wish to present to the class the following day. Pertaining to their new years resolution-make sure to remind them about the three levels to follow. They were making pictures that they could post in the bulletin board and I would pick only three from each group and the over-all winner will get a bag of candies.

10:00 – 10:15 – recess

10:15 – 11:00 - Arithmetic – Ask the students to clear their desk and distribute and empty plastic cup to everyone. Then, distribute a scoop of red dry beans to each student, and a scoop of white dry beans as well. Make the students count 12 of the red beans and to put it in a plastic cup that you distributed earlier. Tell them to put 4 white beans and ask them the total count in the cup by now. Then ask them to remove the white beans and ask them how much is left in the cup. After practicing this for some 15 minutes, then give them a written test on subtraction. Ask them to exchange papers and correct their work. Collect their work.

11:00 – 12:00 – Writing – Demonstrate on the board the difference between script (Italic) penmanship compared to the regular way they were taught to write. Ask them to copy a page from a book using the script writing. Collect their work.

12:00 – 12:30 - Lunch

12:30 – 1:00 – free period; they can play cards, board game or do their homework as long as they are quiet while doing their own thing.

1:00 – 2:00 - Social Studies - ask the students to draw a map of the USA by copying the sample that you will hang on the board. Show them the part that covers the west coast and the east coast. Then ask them where they wish to live after they finish college and why.

2:00 – 2:15 – clean up; place everything in the right places and prepare to go home

ENDURING UNDERSTANDING

The students were given a free hand to choose their career and to understand the importance of sticking to their ambition.

The teacher trained the students to love the art of learning cited specifically with the study of the map and count of the beans. A life full of invigorating activities will produce a willing learner and a successful citizen with a purpose in life.

I don't know if you heard the song by Judy Garland that goes like this: "somewhere over the rainbow, skies are blue, and the dreams that you dream really do come true, someday I wish upon a star etcetera….."

It is a must that you make your students feel good every time they leave your classroom. Make them believe that it was worthwhile getting up in the early chilly morning to go to school to water their garden of learning.

SAMPLE 13 - LESSON PLAN

This lesson plan was written by a high school teacher

Period 1 – Reading Workshop

See page 67 of the workbook – test your grammar. Ask the students to do the exercises orally. After reading the sentence, ask the students to correct the mistakes and read each sentence correctly and with expression.

See page 67 Section C. Read the questions silently. Choose one topic and answer the questions on paper as seatwork.

Period 3 & 5 – English with a Smile

Teacher should discuss the main idea of the story, "Believe in yourself". Describe a time in your life when someone or something helped you to become more confident. Give some reasons why people have little confidence. How can people develop self-confidence? Why is it important to give kind words to everyone? How come some people could be very confident and some are not? Collect journal entries.

Period 6 – ESL 3

Students read silently. Free reading for 30 minutes. Students could read their own book or choose one from the room. Then, each student should discuss the main idea of the story that they read.

CHALLENGE

The students were given free hand to express themselves.

It is important to make the students believe that they matter. Make them believe that they are the shaper of the future generation. Mother Teresa of Calcutta had inspired the little children in India to be kind and happy.

She made sure to feed the little children with kind words each day, hugging them and making them feel that she cares. Mother Teresa is known to be generous with kind words for kind words, (according to this soon to become a Saint) can be short and easy to speak, but their echoes are truly endless.

SAMPLE 14 - LESSON PLAN

This lesson plan was written by a special education teacher – age range of the students 3-5 years old.

Dear Substitute: This might be an unusual assignment for you. Thanks for coming. My students are all physically handicapped. One of them wears a neck brace to keep his head from falling down. Some have very low vision and some are paralyzed. Some are deaf-mute and you may have to use sign language to be able to communicate with them.

Your work for today is enumerated below:

Feed them when they are hungry. In the kitchen, open the refrigerator and you will find ziploc bags with their names on it representing the food of each one of them. Feel free to give them enough for a certain time so that the food can be spread to the end of the day.

Feel them if they are wet (wear gloves please) and change their diapers as needed. Take them to the toilet if needed to doo-doo and to shi-shi. Take them for a stroll under the tree during recess. You have 3 TA's to help you do all these work. After recess, do finger painting. Distribute paint and paper for their use. Bring them to the cafeteria/auditorium to watch a program. Then back to the room and feed them their lunch. Change some of them and rock them in their chairs or bed.

After 30 minutes, it is playtime. Make them play with the computer where they can press buttons to click on different colored lights.

- Some of the students are strapped to a table. Help them to stand and swing the table to make them appear to be in standing position. They take turns being strapped and in standing position for half an hour or so. Allison loves to sleep at this time and while sleeping she keeps smiling – same with James and Timmy. They respond with a smile when rocked.

Brush their teeth without water. Make them watch a video till its time to go home. Parents will be waiting outside.

Thanks for subbing for me.

CHALLENGE

Feel that each one of us is worthy of happiness. This was a challenging day for me being exposed to the many sufferings I have seen of children of young age.

If people will only realize the gifts they have of being able to use their limbs and to be able to stand, to hear, to talk, to see, to be able to function without help-these are gifts that should not be taken for granted.

The kind words and care you give to these children would make them smile and appreciate your presence. It is a challenge I know but the reward echoes to the end of the day.

Pleasant words can make us smile as we face the day, and can make us frown if not given to us. . It is a healing medication that cuts deep into our heart. :

SAMPLE 15 -LESSON PLAN

This lesson plan was written by a high school teacher.

All periods - Make your own autobiography following the outline below:

>   My Family
>   -Who is in my family (include grandparents)
>   -Tell about each of them
>
>   My Childhood
>   -Interesting events I remember
>   -Think about these events
>>   - Why do I remember them?
>>   - Did they teach me a lesson?
>
>   ❖My History
>   -Personal life
>>   - Was I ever punished for something I did not do?
>>   - Things I did at home.
>
>   -School
>>   - School subjects
>>   - Sports
>>   - Awards (attendance, art, contests, etc.)
>
>   Personal feelings
>   - Likes (TV shows, food, clothing, etc.)
>   - Dislikes (TV shows, foods, clothing, etc.)
>
>   My Future
>   -What do I hope to do when I graduate?
>>   - Do my hopes fit my abilities? Why or why not?
>>   - How can I reach my goals?
>   -What kind of person do I want to become?
>>   (honest, gentle, rough, dependable, etc.)

COLLECT THE WORK OF THE STUDENTS AND LEAVE IT
ON TOP OF THE TABLE.

ASSESSMENTS

A good way to get to know the students was to make them work on their autobiography. This would help the teacher gear the student to the right pathway to follow not only with their actions but with their thoughts.

Negative thoughts could linger into our brains and this will affect our future. Punishments given to one in his early age can ruin good relationships be it with parents or friends. It could plan a seed into our life; whether it will help us or destroy us would depend on how we were taught to accept things.

If one was taught to feel the happiness that surrounds him, success is reachable. When we think of how difficult it is to forget, that is when we should be strong to face the challenge that is given to us. Do not think of bad bitter experiences that happened from long time ago as it will only destroy your ambition.

SAMPLE 16 - LESSON PLAN

This plan was written by a physical education teacher, (high school level)

Towards the end of the school year, I was asked to sub for a Physical Education teacher. The teacher's plan asked me to meet the students in the football field and if it would rain, I should take them to the fitness room instead.

The teacher's instruction (Mr. X) to me was to make sure that everyone is busy and it does not matter whatever machine they wanted to use, I should let them do so. . It could be the treadmill, the barbell, the weights, etc. There was no specific instruction given to each student except to make sure that everyone was busy working on physical fitness and to make sure that they were enjoying what they were doing.

I was also asked to feel free to use any on the machines that I feel comfortable using. After watching the students do their weight lifting, I reached for some weights myself and tried to work on them since the students were busy doing their own thing.

Before I knew it, they were surrounding me, teaching me the right way to lift weights. I could see that they were happy that they were the ones teaching me instead of the other way around. I enjoyed their interest and their display of knowledge in this subject. I praised them and I admitted that I did not realize that weights could be placed in different parts of the body for different function. They felt important and they said to me that if Mr. X will be absent again, they will all make sure to tell him to call me instead of someone else as I was awesome, according to them.

Also, on their way out, they said to me that physical fitness sharpens not only their muscles but their boobs as well.

I enjoyed my day but some of my body parts hurt the following day but it was worth it.

ASSESSMENT:

The only way you get the respect of the students was to make them feel that you are no bigger than them.

Today's students can be very realistic about what they want in a teacher. Using emotional appeals like wanting to be like them is a very friendly persuasion

It can't hurt to make them feel important - that they are smarter than you are. If the situation calls for humility and the students will have the opportunity to display their ability….go for it. It will create a very good impression.

Don't hesitate to ask for advice, let your students believe that you learn from them as well.

Continuous learning is a must if you want to win the game.

SAMPLE 17 - LESSON PLAN

This lesson plan was written by a middle school teacher

Periods 1, 3, 5 – ESL (English As A Second Language) – Give a lecture on the word "You". Tell them that YOU is a pronoun and it may refer to one person or more than one.

Always say "you are" or "you were". Never say "you is" or "you was".

Examples: The man told YOU
YOU did not tell me
I will send YOU flowers.
YOU were late
YOU are a good sister.

Ask them (one by one) to come forward and write on the board their own example.

After familiarizing themselves with all the examples given, ask them to do a composition exercise using 10 or more YOU in a story. Give them 15 minutes to do this.

Period 2 – free period

Period 6 – English – Write on the board : Don't be too fast to see evil in others; first look at yourself. Have the students write a two page essay or story touching on the above subject.

ENDURING UNDERSTANDING

There were many instances in the school that could make the students prejudge their classmates. One could be a loner and has no friends. Words fly out from everyone that he/she is weird and maybe crazy. Another student could be well dressed all the time and very popular in the campus, not knowing that all her clothes are hand-me down from her five sisters and she never wore a new dress that was not used first by her sisters.

One student rides a police car to go to school and words fly out that she is brought by her probation officer everyday to school because she had to go back to a house arrest, not knowing that the officer in the police car was her father who takes her to school everyday..

There are many things one could do instead of trying to beat up people with their negative thoughts of someone – just so they could build up themselves.

SAMPLE 18 - LESSON PLAN

This lesson plan was written by a grade 2 teacher.

After checking the attendance and morning activities, write on the board the following words: problem, solution, question, demand, inquire.

Ask them to write these words in 2 ways. Follow it the way it was written on the board and do it also in cursive writing. Require the students to use a ruler to form 2 columns to be able to separate the cursive words from the printed words.

Then ask the students to form themselves into 4 groups. Call out numbers 1 to 4 and all 1s will be on one group, the 2s on the second group and so on.

After forming four groups, ask them to pick up the four dictionary at the back of the room and look for the definition of these words.

Then the sub should give the students lessons on how to use them in a sentence. Make sure that the students understand the examples that you would give as their homework. Tell them to give 2 sentences for each word.

Recess

Call out the words written on the attached paper and give a spelling test.

Play Bingo (you will find it under my table) and give chocolate bar to the winners.

Lunch – Take the students to the cafeteria and leave them there.

After lunch take the students to the library for computer lessons. Mrs. X will take over but don't leave the library. Wait for the students and take them back to the classroom.

Tell them to get ready to clean up before dismissal.

I hope you will enjoy my students!

ENDURING UNDERSTANDING

It was wise of this teacher to train his students how to use the dictionary at an early age.

Familiarizing them to the use of a dictionary would be a great way to learn. Students would realize for themselves that new words will always pop up into their lives. To be able to use it in a sentence is the best way to make sure that the words will not be forgotten.

I remember when I first came across the word dilly-dally. I had to look it up right away and must have used the word some 3 or 5 times in one day.

SAMPLE 19 - LESSON PLAN

This lesson plan was written by a grade 4 teacher.

Start the day with daily announcements from the office. Most of the teachers were at a workshop in the library. I hope the children behave well today, but I do have some with special problems. They are marked on the enclosed class list.

You do not have to do everything as I planned which was all written on the board, but please try to do most. Be firm in your expectations. We have classroom rules. If the children as a whole were active and rude, punish all at one time, i.e. no recess...all stay with heads down.

Individual problems could be handled by talking to them making them write a letter on a folder paper apologizing for their actions, or send them to the office. If the misbehavior involves hurting others, take them to the office.

Simon is a medication child but he is not on it presently. He is talkative and not always in a cooperative mood especially on days with substitutes and changes in routines.

To make things exciting, tomorrow is his last day as he is transferring. He would probably just sit in his chair, include him, invite him to participate and help him if you can, but if he is not accepting your help, then leave him alone. If he walks out of the class and stays by the classroom wall, check on him once in a while.

Once he leaves the premises of the classroom, he has technically run away. Send a note to the office that Simon had left the classroom without your permission. They would send someone down for him. You have the other 25 students to watch and cannot be chasing him around.

Follow the lessons that I have written on the board.

8:30   Language and Spelling (call out the words from my plan)
10:00   Math
        recess and lunch and stay in the cafeteria during lunch
12:30   Literature
1:00   Art
1:45   Library Visit
2:15   Dismissal

CHALLENGE:

This is a very organized teacher and really wanted to be fair with everyone of her students. However, at times, it is really difficult to please everyone.

I tried my best to be patient with Simon and encouraged him to simply do some drawing in his desk but he gave me the f--- 4 letter word. I ignored him and pretended not to hear what he said. He walked out but before doing so he yelled some dirty words before standing outside the classroom wall.

I still controlled my temper. I did not want to end up regretting what I might do. In my old age, I learned not to do what I might regret to do as I cannot undo what I have already done.

I also remember what my grandmother used to tell me that if I cannot say anything good, I should not say anything at all. In other words, she said: SHUT YOUR MOUTH!.

SAMPLE 20 - LESSON PLAN

This Lesson Plan was written by a Middle School Teacher.

I received a call from the Department of Education to sub for a teacher that I know personally and is a friend of mine. I usually get my teaching assignment the night before but since the school was nearby and the teacher is a friend, I agreed to come although I have just taken a pill for my headache that same morning.

I reached the school at exactly 8 AM in time to check with the office and be at my classroom before the student arrived.

There was no lesson plan prepared which I did not mind because my teacher friend warned me to the effect – that she did not get the chance to write one but she was giving me a free hand on what to teach as long as it will deal with Language Arts.

This was not a problem for me because I had been used to teach this subject anyway. The first period went well and the students were all well behaved.

When Period 3 came, a certain student who we shall call as Kekon insisted that I explain the lesson again to him. I have just explained to the class the said lesson. I asked the others if they understood the lesson and everybody agrees that the lesson was well explained. So as not to be aggravated, I sat next to Kekon and explained the lesson to him once again. Right after explaining the said lesson, he asked me to explain it again and again. When I finally realized that he was playing a game with me, I said to him that I cannot be explaining the lessons again and again.

That was when he said to me: "Why wouldn't you? You get paid to work. He also asked me where I live which I ignored and asked me other impertinent questions. When I mentioned to him that I am jotting down the behavior of each student in the classroom, Kekon said to me: "IF YOU BUST ME, I'LL BUST YOU FIRST".

All other periods went well and all other students were well behaved. I made my report to the teacher and gave a copy to the office too.

CHALLENGE

Some of the students could really aggravate you. Kekon must have some problems of his own and I would like to think that he was just testing my patience.

Having taught for some 30 years, I had been exposed to all kinds of behavior, directly or indirectly thrown to me.

I remember what my grandmother used to tell me when I was a kid that I should not stoop to the level of one that is looking for trouble. She used to tell me that I could always turn my back whenever a playmate would tell me that I am a coward.

If you will not turn your back on a stupid challenge to fight, you are allowing the person challenging you to feel good about himself. Did you lose anything for doing so? No, instead you gave yourself a clear conscience.

Be an example of high integrity. You do not want to see yourself bothered and feel that you should have punched him in the nose. For example, a maniac is chasing a man with intent to kill him. The man passes by and turns to the right and disappears. Then the maniac comes up and asks which way his intended victim went. He said he turned left and by doing this, he saved the life of an innocent man. This untruth is good. Just like when you turn your back to a trouble- maker because you want to make him feel good when you know that he has done you wrong.

One of the greatest compliments you can hear from the hip-hop generations these days is this and I quote: "She is cool, she is awesome".

This point of view can make you feel good that you did not go down with someone who wants to put you down.

The following week, I received a letter from Kekon which was forwarded to me by the teacher. (You can see the hand written letter of Kekon to me following lesson 20).

Dear Mhs. P

I'm very sorry for the headache I caused you for this Pd.. I hope you find it in your heart to forgive me I'm very sorry.

Sincerly

Kekon

PART 3

"CHALLENGE ME PLEASE"

BEING UNDER THE SUPERVISION OF A COMPLETE
STRANGER
IN THE CLASSROOM, IN THE FOLLOWING PAGES YOU
WILL SEE VARIOUS PLANS THAT CAN BE USED TO BREAK
THE MONOTONY OF THE DAY

*It is imperative to remember that a master communicator
can either make his audience smile with enthusiasm
or frown with dismay.*

BREAK YOUR STRESS

When students get to appear bored, it is up to the teacher to save the day by reinforcing a method that would make the students perk up.

The teacher could write in a piece of paper the 50 states in the United States. (or depending on the count of the students in the classroom, if you have only 20, then do 10 states).

Then write and cut into pieces the 10 capital cities of those states, put in a basket or a jar. Then, shake the basket and tell the students that this would be like a lottery. If one student picks California, his partner would be the one that picked Sacramento. Then, they are to work as a team.

If your subject is Social Studies, you could make them write their fruits, (example, pineapple for Hawaii) and any other thing that this place is famous for. Let them confer with each other for about 10 minutes and then make them do a 3 minute presentation in front of the class. They could also dramatize their presentations about the state that they are representing.

The teacher should use her imagination on what would be interesting to talk about, to report on, to present to the class, but make sure that the students work as a team.

DRAWING

The teacher should distribute an outline of a drawing. For example, a garden with roots drawn at the bottom of the paper. Then in a certain corner of the paper, there were leaves hanging. In another corner, there is a big branch of a tree not attached to a tree. At the top of the paper, there is a bird flying and trying to land in a big stone.

Make the students finish this unfinished drawing and make it as interesting as possible which can tell a story on what the picture is trying to convey when exhibited into a museum. Color it and make an artist out of a student. Make the student fall in love with arts and make him realize that he is an artist after all without him knowing it.

The art of teaching the student to be creative may lead into great ambition. It would depend on the teacher to gear one into following the ideas in his mind..

The universe is composed of objects. These objects came from ideas and ideas of the universe are thoughts in the mind, which the mind makes. These objects differ in many ways and these objects are results of mere ideas in the mind. Let us train the students to use ideas as a stepping stone to a great invention.

FOCUS

One way to train the students to be observant was to teach them to focus on an object and with this object ask them to think of ideas that could be produced after focusing on that object. For example: Ask two students to come forward in front of the class. Let us say that we have students A and B.

Ask student B to focus his eyes on the left ear of student A.

After 2 or 3 minutes, ask student B to tell you what came to his mind while he focused on the ear of student A. Student B can really make his mind spin and think of many things that was brought to his attention.

He responded with this: "His ear is like a scooper that makes sound to go straight to his ear drum".

Then another student was called and let us call him student C. When asked what C noticed about the ear of A after focusing on his ear. Student C said: "A's ear looks like a cookie that did not flatten.

So you see, with this lesson on learning to focus, ideas can pop up on anybody's mind and a discussion could lead to a great learning process. It can be fun and will help you to figure out how the mind or thoughts of one could be so different from the other.

GOAL: If students are trained to be observant, they will learn to know the importance of forming ideas which can lead to a discovery that can lead to an invention or a fulfillment of an ambition. It is important that students are trained to have a questioning mind wanting to know what makes a thing ticks.

INVENTION OR AMBITION

Tell your students that the purpose of the school was to provide learning experience and prepare them to face the future.

With this in mind, you can inspire the students with your own ambition and what you planned for your life. This could be an ambition that was realized or not, but up until now, you are still trying to reach for the realization of your dream.

With this introduction, ask your students to picture in their mind what they wanted to be or to invent. You can tell your students that a housewife was good in making stuffed animals. One day, she went to a mall and found a store with lots of stuffed animals. Her mind started to work and she realized that she could be in business by creating stuffed animals but dismantled into pieces. She bought parts to put them together after making the head, the body, the limbs, then the parts were assembled on the right body parts making the animal become one piece. The child that will put this together will feel fulfilled that she made her own toy. So, how about you? What do you want to invent?

What do you want to be? Where are you going after your graduation, after your teen years, after you get married? Make your students sell their ideas.

LET'S PLAY

This method could best be applied to the early childhood students. For example, the use of Bingo. As the teacher call out the numbers from a jar, the students will learn numbers applying them to the right column of the alphabet where it belongs.

The students could learn how to concentrate on columns, numbers, alphabets and the triumph of winning and the agony of defeat.

The students could also use playing cards that the teacher made especially for them. For example: A card will show a drawing of seven apples. On the right hand side of the card is written the number seven. Make some 60 cards and distribute them to your 20 students. Each student would be holding 3 cards in his hands. On the teachers table, the teacher will form 6 columns identified with numbers 1 to 6.

Then tell your students to put their cards on the right column on the table when their numbers are called. For example, number 21 should be under the column number 2 and 33 should be under column number 3 and 18 should be under column number 1 and so on and so forth.

The first one that is without cards on her hand is the winner and will be given a prize which could be a chocolate bar.

NEWSPAPER REPORT

Effective teachers teach different ways of learning. It is important to point out to the students the importance of doing something automatically as a daily routine to improve their daily learning process.

This training can better be applied by reading daily periodicals. Point out to your students that by reading the daily newspaper they can be updated on what is going on around them, their neighborhood and the universe.

When we go to a social events, guests could be discussing on current events be it football, physical fitness, the internet, politics or just plain fashions.

All these topics could be answered by reading the daily newspaper.

Students should be given a guideline on what to take note and what to remember in reading a topic.

First of all, let the student remember the title of the story. Make them give you a summary of the article they read. Ask them to write a brief evaluation of the article they read.

Lately, there is too much emphasis on energy. The high price of gasoline is common discussion around the drinking fountain. If someone ask you how this topic can be related to global warming, what would you say?

With this in mind, the teacher could impart to the students why they should really read the daily periodicals. Isn't that enough reason to entice your students to read the gossips of the world?

SOCIALIZING

What do you do well or enjoy doing? One may say: "I love going to the movies on weekends especially if it is a love story". Another one may say: "I only go if it is historical". And then again, another one may say: "I only go if it will make me laugh".

Each one of us have our own purpose in life. But it is an accepted fact that we all live in a conventional society and we should be mingling with our neighbors. That being the case, it is important to learn the art of socializing. How can we learn this art in the classroom?

The teacher may have the option to give an assignment to the students to bring some cookies and drinks the following day because they will have a party after seeing a movie. The following day the teacher can play a video, be it Cinderella or Rocky or whatever they want to watch. After the movie, ask them to mingle with each other over cookies and drinks and discuss the movie that they saw.

Tell them that you will go around to see how you could help out in improving their bad habits if any, and praise them for their good behavior as the case may be. For example, a student picked up a cookie and did not like it and after a bite, she returned it. Another one used her sleeves to wipe her mouth after drinking a soda. The teacher should also praise one for a good move that she may notice. Example: A student was conversing with her classmates about the movie. Let us call them student A and B. A said to B: "I hate the way the star was portrayed to be a hero when actually he was a thief." B answered: "I did not pay much attention to the star, I like the fact that the producer chose Canada to shoot that picture, It is very natural".

At this point, the teacher can praise B for the positive comment she gave after hearing a negative commentary.

THE BOUNCING BALL

The use of a ball could be practiced in all grade levels and in all subjects. With high school students, the ball could be thrown from one to the other as a prize for being quick to think. The teacher will explain to the students that the ball will be thrown to the student that is ready to name 3 U.S. Presidents.

The topics to be discussed could be written on the board and when one is done the ball may be thrown to the next student who is ready to tackle the following topic written on the board. Students will be on their toes wanting to catch the ball and as a result they are forced to be creative with their answers.

This could also be used by the lower grade level of students. For example:

The student who catches the ball will be given the chance to draw on the board any food they want to eat that day.

The goal is to make the students quick on their thoughts, on their imagination and in answering questions. Practicing this method results in unrestrained thoughts and actions and eliminates self imposed limitation of himself.

In this modern times, brainstorming is a method very much used in higher level of education...wouldn't this be a good preparation for facing higher education and challenges of good employment?

THE CARTOON

Here is a method that can be used by all grade levels.

Make the students draw 12 squares and inside that square, the students may draw 2 persons inside the square with one person asking the other to teach her how to skate.

- Each square will have your drawn characters with the following dialogue::

    o Please teach me how to use roller blades
    o First thing you do is to be able to stand like this
    o Then check your balance if you can move with them
    o Then lift one leg and see if you can make one step

This is only one example, you can draw in squares procedures on how to cook, how to sew a dress, how to paint etcetera.

It is important for the students to have the freedom to express themselves in so many ways. It can be done by creative writing, or by demonstration, by drawing their thoughts, or by shooting a video.

THE COMIC STRIP

The teacher assigns the students to bring a page of their favorite comic strip with the blank inscriptions of what they were saying.

The students will be asked to fill the blank circle of their thoughts to produce a story out of the pictures they see in that page. You will notice that each student will have his own version of what was going on or what went on out of that comic page.

Here, the students will learn to give their own uncontrolled opinion of the story they want to tell. Also, this will help the teacher decide on who is funny in the class, the serious one, the introvert and the extrovert, and of course the one with an upbeat personality.

THE FAMILY PICTURE

Ask the students to bring their family picture. Each picture will be shown to the class for them to see what they see in the picture. For example, in this picture, I see the Mother to be very authoritative and confident in her ways and in her thinking. I see the Father to be gentle and easy going. I see him to be humble and hard working. I see Albert's sister to be funky and modern. She seems to like nice things and seems to be a show-off. Albert (who is the student that brought the picture) is the timid kind. He seems to idolize his father and would like to follow his footsteps.

Then, another student will present his family picture and do the same thing done with Albert. Each student will show his own family picture and later on you can ask the particular student how true was the judgment given to each family member and make a tabulation on the board of those who received good judgment and those who received the complete opposite or wrong judgment from the students.

This method will train the students to be observant of each picture that they see and to form their own conclusion out of the picture presented to them.

> This method may also be used with the Grades 1 to 3 level by asking them to bring a picture of themselves when they were infants. Ask them what they were doing when this picture was taken and why it was taken. For example, Mom bathing the baby (the baby being the student that brought the picture named Ashley) and the baby was crying. Ashley would explain to the class that she was forced to take a bath and was promised to be given an ice cream afterwards. The students will take turns in showing their baby pictures and later on if there is more time, each student can add more to the story given earlier. Students will learn to be spontaneous in their thoughts and be prepared to open their mouth and tell the truth.

THE USE OF A TICKING TIMER

The teacher should be holding a 60 second timer on his hand or may be using the wall clock with 60 second timer. If it is a hand held timer, the teacher should pass the timer to a student and make this student be the signal giver on when to start and when to stop.

The teacher would be the one to give the topic to be described by the students.

For example: Describe your shoes in 60 seconds. Describe the ceiling of this room.

You can also make it challenging by describing a very tiny object like your thumb in 60 seconds or a pin, or a winder of a watch etc.

This can be a good preparation to make the student be imaginative in his thoughts and be quick to respond to a challenge.

Timer may be used in different methods of teaching. In the past, it is used to test the speed of the subjects shorthand and typing. Nowadays, it is used not only in the school but also in the office, at home (in baking a cake, in baking a turkey), most of all it is used to test your ability to perform at such a short notice.

Therefore, it would be wise to make the students get use to the ticking timer in their early age.

WRITING A STORY IN SEQUENCE

In writing a story, whether it be for a newspaper or for your personal record, it is important to observe the following sequence.

First of all, a lead paragraph could be emphasized answering the 5 W's. They are: who, where, what, when, why. Then, you can follow with important and interesting facts that you wanted to convey.

This assignment could be given to students of all grade levels depending on the simplicity of the topic for the lower grade level.

For the higher grade level, the students could be asked to write a story that lingers into their mind whether it be religious, political, or historical.

With a partner, a student may discuss this with him/her in preparation for a discussion or conversation that can transpire in a social gathering.

Practice doing this method as often as once a week

THE VIDEO

There will be times when it would be difficult to find a sub that can teach a vocational subject like Electronics or Automotive.

In this case, the teacher may use a video tape related to the subject that he teaches.

Example: In Automotive, the Video tape can show the instructions on how to change oil.

He can video tape himself while he change the oil of his own car.

This can be very appealing to the students and you can be very sure that no one will be sleeping in the classroom while this is played especially so if the teacher will tell the sub to inform the students that when he gets back, they will be tested on the oil change procedure.

****

On the subject of Electronics, the regular teacher can video tape of himself splitting wire to make the students learn how to lengthen a wire that may be too short. There are lots of procedures that can be shown or demonstrated with the use of a Video camera. Make use of them to be able to find a sub that will not say "no" to an assignment given him/her.

DRAMA

Take the students to the cafeteria or auditorium where you could teach them DRAMA. There is a enough space to move around in any of this location to be able to do this lesson on DRAMA.

Tell your students to choose a partner. Ask the students to stay next to their partners. Then ask them to form a circle. Blow your hand and clap three times.

Now that you are sure that everyone is awake then ask them to confer with their partners for 2 to 3 minutes (ask them to guess what one is doing while the other partner will do the opposite. – face each other in circle. while you do this. For example, one student is wiping her cheeks appearing to be crying while the partner keeps laughing.

The partner therefore will do the opposite of what his partner is doing. Another example is that of one appearing to be talking (no sound) while the partner put her finger across her lips appearing to zip up her mouth.

Think of other actions that can be done without sound. Make some 5 actions for every couple. Give yourself a hand for a job well done as you learned the art of pantomime.

After this, keep your circle but not facing each other anymore. Your teacher will call out a volunteer to go to the center of the circle. Your teacher will be the one to start the game telling the volunteer what to do. For example, play dead or make the sound of a goat or a cat or a dog etcetera. With these examples, the students may now start telling volunteers (who are taking turns to be in the center) just what to do.

The volunteer may also lift up something heavy and say : I am an animal and I can lift heavy stuff.. Who am I? Answer: Elephant

All other volunteers should do things with action. This is a fun lesson to do especially on a rainy day.:

THE POSTER

The teacher can fashion a picture made by the class. Have the students form a circle and in the center is a big poster.

Tell the students that this circle symbolize the unity of the group. Tell them the importance of being united as this is the first step to be a team player. Give them ideas on what to do with the poster like drawing a town devastated by a hurricane. Another idea is that of a shopping mall. Tell them that with the first example, A, B, & C students could be in charged of doing the sky the, the clouds, the wind etcetera. D, E & F may be in charged of drawing the houses and so on and so forth. Consequently, they cannot use these examples that you cited. They have to think on their own what they want to work on.

Distribute different colored markers to all of your students. Make them sit down for a few minutes and allow them to confer with each other on what to do with the poster. After some 10 minutes or so, make them go to the center and approach the poster and work on their project. This project may last for an hour or two or it may even take them half a day to finish the project. When you do this, point out that you will be watching their behavior and participation making sure that everyone is participating and that they work as a team.

When they finish their work, do not point out errors in case you are not satisfied with the finish product. Do not try to be on the alert to discover gaps, and bad shadings.

The picture that they might present to you may be imperfect and subject to improvement.

It is important to remember that these students have sought to answer a solution to a project given to them. You, as a teacher, should ponder what interest them and how they perceived the idea that they worked on. A certain portion of the drawing may not even fit the picture. That is not for you to conclude. The idea is that you made your students worked as a team. Thus, in real sense, you, as a teacher have attempted to train the mind of great thinkers.

THE VERBS

As the teacher gives a lecture on grammar, particularly the use of verbs, you as a teacher can assign two students to come forward in front of the classroom to demonstrate this lesson to the class.

What will be the role of the two students? One on the left will give the definition of the verb that is introduced. The other student on the right will demonstrate the verb that is introduced.

For example: To jump. The student on the right will be jumping up and down and the student on the left will define the word jump. Then the teacher on the center will continue the lecture on this word leading to the past and the future tenses like jumped, will jump, jumping etcetera.

You can use this method also in the study of foreign language. Use various words and examples to make sure that you are understood and that the students enjoy learning the difference between the past and the future and the other parts of speech in the study of grammar. It is kind of fun to learn ideas with action. It is nailed into our mind.

PARTY TIME

Originally, I thought of using this method only for the kindergarten students as they are still babies and the young children are known not to keep grudges on anyone.

Why did I say that? Because this method could hurt some students and may refuse to participate in this lesson for feeling inferior for the actions that he will do in following the process that the teacher may require of them.

Also, I realized that some of the young adults are guilty of doing many of the bad examples cited below. With this in mind I came to a conclusion that it would be wise to switch to another approach of picking the students that will do the right and wrong move.

Now, let's party! Pick half of the class to do the bad move and half of the class will do the right move. For example: Three or four students will mingle with the other students as they all eat and drink as they go around the room. The students assigned to do the bad move will chew their food with open mouth which is not right (the right thing to do is to chew your food with mouth closed). The bad movers will also chew their food with noise like chewing gum with wide-open mouth. The good movers will chew their food quietly and closed mouth. In the other corner of the room there are four or five students conversing with each other and while they do so, one of them (the bad mover) will pick his nose while another will pick filthy substance under her nails (bad move).

In another corner of the room, one student will be reading a newspaper. Let's say she is reading the front page. The other student (bad mover) will try to flip the page to the sports section to read her favorite column. Although she tried to read only a portion of the news as the paper was folded by the front page reader, this is still a bad move.

Here is another example. The students would be invited to a buffet table. The students would pick up their own plates to fill them with their choice of food. One bad move would be to try to break the line and skip his turn to be able to be ahead of the line. These are simple moves but may not be taught from home especially if their parents do not know any better or if their parents have no time to teach them as they are working parents who have no time for their children.

You can think of other good and bad move and show to your students the difference between right and wrong. After this session, no one will really feel inferior or ashamed because the teacher assigned them their moves. It is not something to feel inferior about because it was required of them to demonstrate to the class for the benefit of everybody.

SAVING FOR THE RAINY DAYS

Nowadays, our children do not know the value of money. They believe that since they can always ask their parents to support their needs, then they should not bother to worry as to where the money is really from.

Thus, it is time to open the eyes of your students to learn how to spend the money they earn and how to budget their income after graduation.

Make some dollar bills out of some colored papers. Mark the red ones as $10 dollars, the yellow ones as $5 dollars and so on and so forth. Then, distribute them to your students, giving each one of them a total of $1,000 each. (Tell them to be creative as the student who will save more will get a prize).

$1,000.00 is their paycheck for one month. Out of that one month, they have to pay the following monthly bills:

$450.00	house rent
30.00	phone bill
50.00	electric bill
100.00	public transportation expense
220.00	food expense
50.00	miscellaneous
100.00	to savings account
$1,000.00	TOTAL

If this is followed to the penny, you can look forward to a $1,200 savings annually. On the other hand, if you find a room-mate that can split the expenses with you then, you can look forward to a bigger savings to be deposited to your bank account.

Students should be taught how to handle their money and to make sure to save for the rainy days as the sun is not always shining especially during the winter season.

PART 4

GUIDELINES TO "REACH FOR THE STARS"

*After graduation, the student will enter a new field
which is that of finding employment. He has to learn to
be independent now. Understanding his version of good and
bad will be his guideline as he goes on finding his place in
this society that is full of trickery.
After learning the distinction between good and bad
from both his teachers and/or his parents.
it is imperative now that he accepts the idea that his action
is a product of his free will which can lead to a better or bad existence
of himself. A child is free to build his
ideals and/or to risk all on their realization. After justifying his
action, whether it be good or bad, he rises up to say:*

**" I am the master of my fate,
I am the captain of my soul".**

Now, let us flip the following pages to reach for the stars.

PICTURE TAKING

Get ready to learn to look your best. Study yourself in front of the mirror and check on your best angle.

You heard the term "photogenic". Everyone could be photogenic if you gave yourself a good check-up on what is your good and bad angle. Be honest with yourself.

In my younger days, I enrolled in a School Of Theater Arts. Picture taking was a must and when I faced the camera, my teacher said to me..."Wilhelmina, you look like a cake"

I was in my teen years then and of course I was hurt and ashamed because she said to me that I look like a cake in front of all my classmates.

My teacher took me to another room full of mirrors and asked me to study myself and check on my best angle. I was completely free in that room and after looking at myself again and again, I realized that I really look like a cake. I started moving around the mirror and checked on my best angle. I have a round face and in my teen years, I was a bit chubby. After moving my face to the left, to the right, up and down, I finally discovered my best angle. I was given an hour to study myself in front of the mirror and after an hour, my teacher came back and asked me to pose.

What a big difference. The teacher never stopped saying…."beautiful, beautiful". From that time on, I don't feel ashamed anymore if I am corrected as I know that it is for my own good when a negative thought is thrown to me. I make sure to think that I can easily turn that negative thought to a positive one as it is a cue for me to shift my focus to my positive outlook.

You will see a sample of the pictures in the next page after I was asked to study my best angle in the other room

THANK YOU!

A thank you note is not enough to express your thanks for an act accorded to you. What do I mean by that?

Let me tell you a story that needed to be told as a sign of appreciation as it lingers in my mind up until now.

At the age of 21, I left home to start a new life on my own. I realized that I do not have enough money to be independent as yet. But my fighting spirit is great that deep inside me, I could hear voices that I would make it after all.

I asked for the help of an elderly friend who acts like a father to me to help me find a room to rent. He tried to help me but since he himself is not financially stable as he depends on his wealthy wife to provide for him, and so he asked his wife without my knowledge to give him $100.00 to be able to pay for a hotel room for me while he helps me find a job. I overheard the wife yelling at him for helping me but she gave in and handed him $100.00 after lecturing on him and making him promise to stop helping people.

Luckily, I found a job, the following day and so I promised my friend that I would pay him as soon as I get paid. He told me not to bother. I did not keep a grudge on his wife for her unwillingness to help. I just said to myself that if I were in her shoes, I would probably do the same. To cut the story short, my friend died after 6 years and his wife became my best friend up until now as I always remember to thank her for helping me out in my time of need.

I never gave up on her. I know that I owe her something. Since I cannot repay my deceased friend, I made sure to repay his wife with an endless thanks.

RESUMÉ

Start typing your name in the top center of the paper followed by the following information: address, telephone number and email address.

The next information you have to give is your qualification summary. Start with the most recent experience. Next heading will be your community development experience. (Make sure to type the headings in capital letters). You can say for example: I was a volunteer worker for YMCA as a life guard during summer time. Think of what you have done for your community where you contributed something to help them.

Then, the next topic will be your educational background followed by your professional experience if any.

If this is your first time to enter the field of employment, specify more personal traits of yours that will make you stand out from the rest of the applicants.

You may also add 3 references and their phone numbers. However, I will not suggest that you do this if your professional experience is long enough to speak for yourself.

MOTIVATION

Motivating the students to pick an art can be a chore. However, by citing past experiences that the teacher may have first hand information in this matter will help the teacher to succeed in accomplishing this goal.

For example: My niece who have just finished her 4 year degree in Sports Medicine wanted to work on her graduate course at a certain university in San Jose, California. She was accepted with a condition that she has to enroll in any art subject before the start of the school year. Why so? Because, the school believes that all work with no play can ruin a good mind.

She enrolled as required and loving it now that she learned a good past time to break the monotony of serious research work. Another example that I could tell you is the time that I was pushed by my mother, at the age of 6, to learn how to play the piano. I did not like the idea of breaking the habit of playing with my neighbors at certain hours after school. But then, she bribed me with toys and sweets if I will try to learn how to play. In the beginning, I detested it but as I was given more peppy tunes by my teacher, I looked forward to master a piece so that I will be given a new lesson. I could hardly wait for the time when my teacher would come and give me another peppy tune until I learned to challenge myself and get to like playing other tunes. From the age of 6, up until now I find it delightful to play the piano and it becomes a soothing moment to break the monotony of my daily grind. I remember going on a cruise to Japan some years ago, I found myself not being able to sleep one night so I walked down to the recreation room and found a grand piano sitting there. I tried to tickle some keys and ended up playing "O Sole Mio". As I got up, an elderly man at the back of the room started clapping his hands saying "anchor...anchor". He was blind and so I walked towards him and he said to me.."I have been all over the world and had been to concerts and symphonys but have never heard a simple tune played with too much emotion." I shook his hands and thanked him for making my evening so memorable. Playing a musical instrument can make you stand out from the crowd. You can be the light of a party and be noticed even if you are not the most beautiful person in the room. Another incident that happened to me was this. I was invited to a birthday party of a 9 year old child. There was a piano in the room. So, I offered to play "happy birthday" as she blew the candles on her cake. After the music, the girl asked her mother to hire me to teach her play the piano. I did not want to do it but after looking at her almost begging me to say yes...she started jumping up and down and promised me that she will be a good student. I agreed to teach her for no more than 3 months. She now plays by ear and would invite me now and then to listen to her music. She is now a young adult.

There are so many ways you can motivate your students. Take a look at item 8 of lesson 6 in this book. The idea of breaking the monotony of a daily task is best expressed by the introduction of recess time. *ALL WORK AND NO PLAY MAKES JOHN A DULL BOY.* A teacher, just like your parents, should help and motivate the children to grow, just as the gardener helps the flower to grow. You would be helping him to adjust himself to a society in which his social and individual experiences would both be helpful in the development of his complete personality.

If the child refused to be disciplined, it is the duty of the teacher and or the parents to come into the picture and play the part of making the child a civilized being. For example, if a boy that is in his teen years insists on wearing a beard that makes him look like a gangster, he should be exposed to other case studies in the past showing proofs of those teens who are in juvenile jail that looked exactly like him. Make him realize that he lives in a conventional society that should not be ignored, nor should the child be educated in complete disregard of the values of society.

It is important to remember that the purpose of education is to train and mould individuals to contribute to the good of the whole.

JOB HUNTING

A typical job position that the young graduates look for is that of being a secretary, a receptionist, a clerk or a front office person. It seems like positions of this level is a good stepping stone to get the company to hire you.

Let us say that you applied for a job as a secretary for a printing company. Your main duty in this small company with a staff of 4 people is to make sure that invoices are made and collected on time as transaction occurs.

However, at times, you find yourself bored as business is slow. There is no one that promotes the business and look for new clients except the owner himself. On the other hand, the owner seems to be busy with other personal matters on his hand.

You have a type A personality that you find yourself always wanting to do something. What then can you do in this scenario? The answer is simple. Pick up the phone and start calling companies that can possibly use some printing jobs for their business like restaurants. You can tell them that you can print receipts for them that may give them the chance to win a free dinner in their next visit by making sure to find 3 stars printed next to the total amount of their tab. Once you succeed in doing this, then that would be the time to talk it over with the owner. Ask him/her if this idea of yours is okay with him. When he agrees then that would be the time to give him your surprise contact (which you can always cancel on the other end should the boss says no). It is very likely that this contact you made will give you an open door for a higher position in the company. Good luck!

INTRODUCE YOURSELF

Time will come when someone would ask you to introduce yourself. This could be done by giving your name and that's it.

However, in different situation, you will be asked to introduce yourself in front of an audience and that is when you could be challenged on what to say.

You cannot just say your name and sit down. This will be the time to make sure that you will be remembered after you get off the podium. How do you do it?

Think of something about yourself that will make you outstanding to your audience. For example you can start by questioning your audience in this form:

"How many of you have 2 hands? Raise them up, (the audience will raise up their hands) and as they raised them, ask them what they call the face of their hands.

You will hear them reply: "palm". Then, you can say, my name is Palmer. Many of my friends wanted me to read their palms but once I say $50.00 per reading, then they look away and play deaf. I hope you will not play deaf as I really charge only a dollar. Then you can continue to say more depending on how comfortable you are in front of your audience. Your goal is to be remembered with a smile in their face as you leave the podium.

INTERVIEW

There are various ways of being interviewed. The typical interview is when you walk in to an office to be interviewed for a job you are applying for.

Another way is to be interviewed by phone by one person or a panel.

Another way is the informal approach where you will find yourself invited to a neutral place like a coffee shop to be interviewed where the employer can also check your knowledge of your social skills.

This topic will be better explained if I give you my personal experiences in the course of my job hunting. One time, I received a call from a secretary telling me to expect to be interviewed by her boss in about 2 hours. She wanted to make sure that I was home in preparation for this interview and so I said that I will look forward to his call. Right on time, he called and asked me right away this question: "what do you think of ugly people"? I was shocked as I was not expecting to be asked such a question.

I had to pause for a while and had a drink of water and I replied: "In the first place, I do not believe there is such thing as ugly person; somehow, there is something beautiful in a person. It could be his hands, his eyes, his skin, more so with this modern extreme makeover through plastic surgery and let us not forget that beauty may come also from the inside. One could have a beautiful physical attribute but deep inside him is full of selfishness and negative thoughts." Then I added that if one is ugly now it is his choice to be so.

And so, as you see, when you are interviewed expect the unexpected. A typical question that could be asked of you is this: "why should I hire you?" This is the time to sell yourself and make sure that you tell him what he wants to hear.

SOCIAL SKILLS

Children should also be taught social skills from their teachers. In this hip hop generation, parents are always jumping from one appointment to another not having the time to teach their children social skills that is a must to practice in a booming society.

Abraham Lincoln met a kid in the park and the kid greeted him "good morning Mr. President" In turn, the president said: "good morning young man"!. The secret service agent surrounding him asked him "Sir, why do you bother to greet that young kid"? Abraham Lincoln replied: "because I do not want that kid to think that the president of the United States does not know how to say "good morning"!

It is important to utter positive phrases like saying: "Thank you for seeing me at such a short notice......, It was good to see you......, I enjoyed meeting you......, Thank you for coming......., I am happy to see you......I look forward to seeing you again".

Children should be taught to appreciate the joy of making others feel good with their presence. If there is a doubt in your mind that you might not enjoy the company of the people in the social event that you will go to, just make sure to have enough words of good will in your pocket where it is easy for you to reach and be ready to throw those words of good will before you make your quick exit.

The most successful people are those who have mastered good social skills. They usually rise to any occasion. Your ability to communicate well with your positive attitude will make a better YOU.

HOW DO YOU SEE YOURSELF

Are you an outgoing person or a loner? Do you consider yourself to be the life of the party or a bore?

If you have a chance to work for a company, will you consider yourself a contributor or a follower of instructions?

Depending on how you evaluate yourself will make or break you. Do not forget that above all things, you should respect yourself if you want others to respect you.

For example you can start with this statement:

"You can count on me to be there at 12 noon and not 12:01 when you asked me to be there to meet you because I am a very reliable person. You can always count on me to be on time. I make sure to give more than I can take. Anybody that knows me will assure you that they have high regard for my opinion when asked to break a tie on certain vote".

This is an example of what you can say of yourself when asked.

141

DRESS UP OR DRESS DOWN

Depending on where you are going, it would be best to dress down than dress up. For example, you cannot go to a job interview with a plunging neckline and a very hugging dress to your body.

I know that hugging outfit is the fashion but as an office worker, you wouldn't want to be the center of attention making the boys look at you and your body instead of focusing their eyes into the computer to meet a deadline.

In going to a social event, it is better to play it safe and wear a skirt and blouse where you can always add accessories or remove them depending on the crowd.

To avoid criticism, wear something that will not make you the center of gossip in your place of work. Depending on the kind of job you do, let your judgment be your guide if you do not want to drown yourself with negative thoughts.

On the other hand, you should also remember that all accomplished persons are victims of countless criticism. Just get out there and meet the reality.

TO TELL A STORY

The teacher should start a story like this: The roaring waives and the blue water makes the sunset more appealing to the eyes of the onlookers. A couple hugs each other as they watched the sun goes down inch by inch. They were making their own memories just by watching the sunset..."now, continue my story Allison", so, Allison picked up the story with this: As the couple watched the sunset the other onlookers have misty eyes as they gaze at their surroundings. A boy came running in with a flying kite. The kite caught the waives and the boy started to look for his father who is across the street. Then, the teacher pointed to the next student to continue the story until all students take turns to put in their two cents into the story.

The teacher should emphasize the importance of a surprised ending... the climax of the story. Training the students to be creative in their imagination is like training them to be a team worker. They learn to think fast, to help each other, to make ready for the future.

The teacher may also give a story as a whole but the teacher may ask the students to change the climax, the ending, or the beginning of the story.

THE END

- Professional and Educational Background of Wilhelmina Pinheiro

1. Licensed Substitute Teacher in Arizona, Hawaii and Rhode Island
2. Holder of Professional Teaching License in the State of Rhode Island
3. Holder of Teaching Certificates in Private Schools in the State of California and Hawaii
4. Holder of Adult Education Teaching Certificate in the State of Hawaii
5. Business Instructor, Heald Business College
6. Fashion and Modeling Instructor, Barbizon Modeling School
7. Seminar Lecturer in the field of Social Grace. Fashion Modeling, Photography

------------------------------------******------------------------------------

*Graduated, Master of Arts in Multi-Cultural Education, University of San Francisco, 1990

*United States Peace Corps Volunteer, Dominican Republic, 2000-2002

*AMERICORPS-Vista Volunteer, Reno, Nevada, 2004-2005

*Trained Teachers on Methodologies of Teaching Dominican Republic and State of Nevada

*Crisis Corps Volunteer – Worked with FEMA and assisted the Katrina and Rita hurricane victims in the State of Texas, 2005

Printed in the United States
49892LVS00005B/406-429